# CAUGHT IN A TRAP

# CAUGHT INA TRAP

## RICK STANLEY
### WITH PAUL HAROLD

WORD PUBLISHING
Dallas·London·Vancouver·Melbourne

CAUGHT IN A TRAP

**Library of Congress Cataloging-in-Publication Data**

Stanley, Rick.
   Caught in a trap / Rick Stanley and Paul Harold.
      p.   cm.
   ISBN 0–8499–0979–1
   1. Presley, Elvis, 1935–1977.   2. Rock musicians—United
States—Biography.   I. Harold, Paul.   II. Title.
ML420.P96S64   1992
782.42166'092—dc20
[B]                                                      92–34808
                                                            CIP
                                                             MN

23459  LB  987654321

*Printed in the United States of America*

To Robyn

She was the first to help me unleash my positive potential. Despite the challenges of being married to Elvis Presley's brother, thank God, she has never looked back.

# Contents

# Introduction

Why another Elvis book? With more than fifty books discussing every aspect of his public and private life, why another? There are exposés, fan books, and picture books, but all of them fail or breakdown at one level: None of them adequately address the why questions that continue to swirl around the paradox that was, and to some extent is, Elvis.

Some may question my credentials. I was one of three brothers to Elvis. That doesn't make me the final authority on Elvis, but I lived with or near him for almost two decades, seven years of which were spent on tour with him. I've had fifteen years to reflect over Elvis's life and to gain the perspective and objectivity that only time can give.

I want to be up front with you right at the start: I'm an evangelist. I became a Christian just two months after Elvis's death. But this book is not a soapbox for me to use to preach to you. I mention my calling because it qualifies me to address life's most important questions—questions like: What's the secret of happiness? Where do I find meaning and purpose in life? How do I meet my needs to love and be loved?

Like most of us, Elvis struggled with these questions. How he answered them for himself is the theme of this book, and, from my perspective as a person committed to helping others solve life's riddles, what Elvis learned and what we in turn can learn from him is the greatest legacy he can leave us.

As you read this book, never doubt my love for Elvis. At the time of his death, he was the most important person in my life. Nothing bothers me more than to hear him ridiculed and demeaned by people who didn't know him personally or who lack compassion for him as a human being whom God loved. But the years have matured my affection and sharpened the focus of the lens through which I now look back at my life with Elvis. As such, I do not gloss over the negative aspects of Elvis's life, as painful as they may be to me personally and especially to the die-hard Elvis fan. He would not want me to do so. Believe me at this point: I was as close to Elvis as a brother could be, and if he were here today he'd say, "Go for it, Ricky. Tell it like it is, man."

Lastly, I hope that this book will help restore a measure of compassion for a man who struggled against great odds in life. He had many successes and failures along the way, and—in spite of his tragic end—he left a cultural legacy of real value to our society. If there were forces beyond Elvis's control (and I believe there were) that "caught" him early in life and held him captive to the very end, then understanding those forces is more compassionate than a glorified treatment that praises the man and perpetuates the myth. If Elvis had known he was going to die that early morning of August 16, 1977, he would have pleaded with his fans to learn from his life the truths that are eternal. This book is an honest effort to grant him what I am convinced would have been his final wish.

Rick Stanley
Fort Walton Beach, Florida

# *1*

---

# The Gift

*M*any times I've imagined what it must have been like the night Elvis recorded his first hits.

On July 6, 1954, Elvis sits, a microphone before him, in the midst of his first recording session. At nineteen, still a kid really, he's as jumpy as his early music will be. He wears small-checked peg pants and a cream-colored shirt, one of those open-collared 1950s numbers with a pocket on either side of the buttons. They've been at this for a while. Elvis's sandy pompadour is already mussed; its d.a. buckshot. After a brutally hot day, the long, narrow recording studio, the home of Sun Records, is like a furnace, and he's sweating, the sides of his face slick and pale. The heat's on . . . in several ways. His dark eyes are haunted by his fears, and his soon-to-be-famous snarling-lipped mouth, with its crooked teeth, bites off short, panting breaths. He looks like a cornered animal.

Sam Phillips, the owner of Sun Records, has asked Elvis and the two musicians working with him—Scotty Moore on electric guitar and Bill Black on standup bass—to record a country ballad, "I Love You Because." They run through the number, once, twice. It drags, speeds up, remains uneven. Elvis serves up the sentimental lyrics with too much syrup, or backs away like a tongue-tied suitor, not selling the song but pushing it—mostly away from him. He talks through the intro the first time, whistles it the next. Elvis cannot decide how he wants to frame his voice, whether he wants to do some full-moon crooning or lay back. Sam

---

cuts off the next take in midcourse. It's not working. He tells the guys to take a break.

Elvis stands up. The next thing he does is a piece of genius. In the next few moments, in a sense, he becomes Elvis. It's the instant of his birth as a great artist. (A similar gambit to the one he's about to employ also makes him a cultural hero.) What does he do? He starts clowning around. Cutting up. Blessed are the goofballs, the crazies, for they refuse to take things seriously.

Elvis takes what looks and feels like an impossible situation, and he changes the rules, the format, and the approach. He turns the game into a different one—a new game, and this one he's good at. (At the end, did he believe too much in the life that he had invented, not seeing how it might be changed?)

He's singing his favorite Arthur Crudup tune, "That's All Right Mama." He has a feel for the song.

> Well, that's all right mama,
> That's all right b-y-ou.
> That's all right, mama.
> Jest anyway you do.

Forty years later we hear immediately what made that nineteen-year-old into ELVIS! He packs most of it into the first line. The shaking tremolo cry that makes the space-filler, "well," into the battle cry of a new hedonistic republic. Those Southern open vowels, *ah ah* ah, that make the line glide. The syncopated drum strokes of the two m's in "mama" that give Elvis a chance to vary the rhythmic pattern, keeping time with his own rimshot articulations. He could sing, boy. He sure could sing.

As the guitar work bounces over the dance floor and the thumping bass rolls it around the corners, the brightness of Elvis's voice expresses an irrepressible good humor. "That's all right," and we believe him.

The mood of the song contrasts sharply with the lyrics. The lover's girl is going away, and his parents don't approve of her, but the lover has not given up hope; he'll settle for whatever last attentions his baby will pay him. He pursues her with a joking good humor that allows them both to back out of the situation with good grace. That's a key. Elvis always took an ironic stance to the sexiness of rock 'n' roll. There was never any cosmic significance to his musical seductions, no deadening (and stupid) seriousness. At the bridge of "That's All Right Mama," he even breaks into happy-go-lucky nonsense syllables, "de de dee de de da, de dee duh."

Elvis flatters with his attentions, and he is vulnerable to rejection, but he makes no demands. He is the perfect fantasy. Millions and millions of women thought so, and in the timeless world of music, they still do. Men are drawn to imitating him and his success rate.

When Elvis stands up and starts fooling with the number, Scotty Moore and Bill Black soon join in. Sam Phillips shoots out of the control booth and asks, "What're y'all doin'?"

"Just goofin' off," Elvis answers.

"Well, back up, and let's see if we can put it on tape," Sam says.

Scotty, Bill, and Elvis run through the song a couple more times, working out Scotty's flourishes and solo, Bill's dynamics. They cut the actual record on the third or fourth take. Now that the session is rolling, Elvis feels an energy he has never experienced before. It is something beyond mere pleasure, or even happiness. He feels like a surgeon who has held his patient's life in his hands and brought him all the way back. He feels like the star football player who, although injured, breaks free on a sixty-yard run in the fourth quarter to fulfill everyone's hopes and win the game. He feels like a preacher mounting his holy mountain and glimpsing the promised land.

I know this feeling, too. It does not come from fame, although it can be confused with fame. And it does not come from within oneself, although there is every temptation to claim it for one's own. It comes from being in the right place and doing what you've been appointed to do, which is at least destiny, if not providence. No matter how hard you work for it—and Elvis worked harder for his moment than many have imagined—it is a gift.

# 2

# Born to Be King

While the U.S. Postal Service's 1993 release of the Elvis stamp may signal to many that Elvis has finally been accepted as a cultural hero, many people in America still regard Elvis with ambivalence. His fans, who are legion, love him unreservedly. But one side of our culture still views Elvis with uncertainty. Their favorite quote about Elvis might well be, "200 million fans can't be wrong," or "He sure loved his mom"—backhanded compliments if there ever were any. It says that they believe that Elvis owes his success to the "average" person's mass taste and insinuates that the elite goes along, but only for its own money-making purposes. Most of us have friends, for example, who may have never read a book about Elvis or purchased any of his records, and yet they consider The Beatles, Bob Dylan, Bruce Springsteen, or even Guns N' Roses to be cultural bellwethers.

Nevertheless, Elvis presents America with a face so closely resembling its own that much of the country can hardly bear to look in the mirror. He has the frontiersman ancestry of Scotch-Irish, with a few pints of American Indian and Jewish blood thrown in, common to much of white America. He was reared in a Pentecostal church. And he was poor. Dirt poor. Not poor in a way that can be romanticized, even though Elvis's family could be thought of as victims. They had limited opportunities and were unable to capitalize on them. In fact, the generations closest to Elvis kept blowing the new chances that presented themselves.

Elvis makes us look at a part of the American experience many of us would like to forget and also at the strange fact that genius can appear anywhere.

On January 8, 1935, Elvis was born in a shotgun house built by his father in the poorest white neighborhood of East Tupelo, Mississippi. His mother, Gladys Smith Presley, gave birth to twins that day, Elvis Aaron and his stillborn brother, Jesse Garon.

The traumatic circumstances of the twins' birth affected Gladys profoundly. Her maternal, protective instincts, her grief, and what must have been a severe case of postpartum depression expressed themselves in her conclusions about the twins' birth. And she instructed Elvis in her beliefs about his birth as if it were a revelation from heaven. Jesse, she said, was his identical twin, and even now watched over the family and protected them. In later life Elvis often felt that Jesse would be equal to any situation that made him feel inadequate, so Gladys's views about Jesse may have convinced Elvis that Jesse was in some way the superior of the two. Perhaps she said something like, "Jesse was too good for this world, and the Lord wanted him beside him right away." Elvis also identified the voice of his conscience with Jesse's speaking to him, so there can be little doubt that Jesse existed for Elvis as an extension of the better side of his nature. Gladys probably never intended for Elvis to make such a conclusion, but children are like wet cement, and Gladys's influence on Elvis was profound.

Gladys played a dominant role in her son's life. When she died, Elvis marked her grave with the quotation, "Not my will but thine." I'm sure that Elvis meant this as a tribute to Gladys's Christian faith, the subordination of her will to Christ's. But some biographers don't think Elvis meant it that way—at least not in his heart. Although in many ways he felt that he lived his life for his mother, especially during the early years of his career, I don't believe Elvis meant the inscription to stand as a pledge of his continuing commitment to *her will*. The phrase comes from Jesus' agony in the Garden of Gethsemane, before his crucifixion. Elvis's reverence for his boyhood faith would have prevented him from misapplying the Scripture so overtly.

Gladys raised her son hardly ever letting him out of her sight. She did not like anyone else touching the baby. Because she had lost Jesse, the naturally protective instincts of any mother were, in Gladys's case, probably exaggerated. The anxiety and grief she must have felt because of Jesse's death no doubt strengthened her parenting resolve and probably contributed to her overprotectiveness (about which so much has been written).

Gladys had an impulsive, highly romantic nature that led her to take three great leaps of faith in her life toward her heart's desire. Everything she did expressed her desire for a better life, and she had reason to want one. She came from a large family of eight children; she was the fourth daughter. Her mother, Doll—a remarkable, pretty, pampered woman—took to her bed early in life. At one time, she had tuberculosis, from which she seemed never to recover fully. As a result, it seems, the rest of the family served her rather than her taking care of them. Gladys's father, Bob Smith, was a share-cropper on one farm and then another. The family moved about every two years in Lee County, Mississippi, always hoping the next place would be a permanent home. Gladys's father was a good-hearted man but a poor farmer. He was, however, good at one thing—moonshining. His stills supplemented the family income enough to keep them all alive, but barely. To his credit, he never went full time into the illegal trade; he preferred respectability to easy gain and labored unceasingly for his family.

Within the family, Gladys was known for her laid-back attitude; outside of it, her polite, "sweet" manner. Nervous, high strung, and prone to irrational fears, Gladys always looked forward to social activities, because they made her feel better.

Early on she manifested an eagerness to acquire things, appearing at the local general store whenever she had any change to buy first a Nehi, then, in a separate visit, snuff, then, appearing once more, a pink barrette, licorice, or peppermint, buying the least expensive items so that she would have as many things as she could. Unfortunately, throughout her life she would exhibit this habit of impulsive buying.

As a teenager, Gladys loved to dance, the kind of dancing known then as "buck dancing," the Charleston and other jazz steps where the partners move opposite one another, not touching, but performing on their own for the other's delight. She loved hearing Jimmie Rodgers and the first Victrolas and his "Corinna, Corinna." Everyone who knew her says that she had rhythm—the sense of freedom she expressed in her dancing became part of local legend. Her wild moves made her popular at local parties. Her dancing seems to have inspired a greater sense of independence and self-assurance in Gladys. She began to take more initiative in several directions.

Working in the fields on Burk's farm, their latest place of residence, Gladys started striking up conversations with a young farmhand. When he picked cotton, she picked along rows close to his. One of their neighbors' daughters noticed this and accused Gladys of pursuing the young man, which precipitated a hair-pulling, face-slapping catfight. Onlookers had to separate them.

Gladys was, in fact, pursuing the young man, and one night they ran off and got married. Their life together remained confined to their elopement, since the young man was already married.

Her father died of pneumonia when Gladys was in her late teens. This meant she had to find a full-time job, something more than the seasonal field work and babysitting she had been doing. Through her church, The Church of God and Prophecy, in Union Grove, Parkertown, she learned that many women her age were going to work in factories and shops in Tupelo. She took a job at the Tupelo Garment Center as a sewing machine operator for two dollars a day in December 1932.

Gladys's uncle, Gains Mansell, shared the pastorate at the First Assembly of God Church in East Tupelo. He and other relatives helped Gladys move her family—a reconstituted collection, including her younger brothers and sister, and her mother— into a house on Kelly Street in an East Tupelo neighborhood, the poorest one, "above the highway." Gladys did well at her work, and her independence helped her to take charge of her life and her family.

Then her romantic nature led her to take a second leap of faith, to pair her fortunes with a young man four years her junior, Vernon Presley. She met him at the First Assembly of God Church. Like Gladys, he came from a share-cropping family. His daddy, J.D., and the rest of their household worked shares on Orville Bean's dairy farm. Although Gladys was now the head of her own household and Vernon was only seventeen years old, they decided to elope. They made this decision so impulsively that they had to borrow three dollars to pay for the wedding license, and they had no idea where they would live. Vernon's own father considered him lackadaisical. Gladys herself understood his lack of ambition. (Caring about his father the way he did, Elvis's early success allowed Vernon to retire shortly after turning forty. Vernon may well have worked harder as Elvis's office manager later in life—a job he did very well—than he ever had during his career as a laborer.) But Vernon was a tall, strapping, blond-headed young man, and the two young people were clearly caught in the grip of passion.

Gladys clearly looked to love—love alone—to improve her life, without thinking concretely about how. The marriage did result in a temporary improvement of her circumstances. The landowner Orville Bean loaned Vernon $180 so he could build the shotgun house on Saltillo Road next to his parents' place, the tongue-and-groove wooden house where Elvis was born.

Then, nervous and high strung as she was, suffering from the trauma of Jesse's loss, Gladys's love for her son became the repository of all her hopes. It's natural for a mother to give herself completely to a newborn infant, and it's equally natural for one who has been through a traumatic double-birth in which one child lived and one died to be more protective and clingy than she might have been otherwise. Vernon's own foolish actions, though, and the sudden return of Gladys's life to a truly precarious poverty kept Gladys's attentions focused exclusively on Elvis and changed the family dynamics permanently.

When Elvis was nearly three, his father, on November 16, 1937, to be exact, was indicted for forgery. Vernon had sold a pig to his boss and mortgage holder, Orville Bean. The farmer wrote him a check in the amount of four dollars. Vernon thought the price was scandalous. Two drinking buddies, Travis Smith (Gladys's brother) and Lether Gable, talked it over with him that night. Passing around the moonshine, they decided Orville Bean wasn't going to get away with it. Either they changed the original check to read fourteen or forty dollars (depending on who is telling the story), or they forged a brand new check, tracing Bean's handwriting from the original onto a duplicate. In any case, they were caught, and Bean, believing he had been charitable to buy the pig in the first place, could not be talked into dropping the charges.

Judge Thomas H. Johnston sentenced Vernon to three years in Parchman, the Mississippi state penitentiary. No one posted Vernon's bail—although his father helped put up the money for Travis Smith—and Vernon was away from his family for the six months between his apprehension and the trial and then for his nine-month stint in Parchman. Community pressure resulted in his sentence being commuted to that term.

Gladys's anger at her husband can be imagined. She suffered through two long winters of privation, dependent on welfare and the charity of her neighbors.

Elvis, after many days of crying fits at his daddy's absence, began to see himself as his mother's protector. He toddled around the house, asking her if she wanted a drink of water or a stool for her "sooties," their baby-talk word for feet. He patted her and said, "There, there, my little baby."

Gladys consoled Elvis and herself in two ways during this time. Mother and son went to the Assembly of God Church every time they opened the doors; her uncle, Gains Mansell, was now the sole preacher. They enjoyed the services, especially the gospel singing, which would lead Elvis to say, more than thirty years later, that gospel singing "more or less puts your mind to rest. At least it does mine, since I was two."

Gladys also began drinking more heavily during this period. She seems to have been a secretive drinker, taking her nips on the sly. Her relatives, particularly Ben and Agnes Greenwood, with whom Gladys and Elvis were staying, noticed the drinking, but felt grateful the moonshine calmed the distraught woman down. Gladys's drinking, no doubt, established the classic pattern of alcoholic dependence on the part of the parent and codependence on the part of Elvis in the Presley household. The denial of this behavior has been so great that many Elvis biographers have looked right at this alcoholic pattern and then veered away. No one has incorporated what we now know about substance abuse and the patterns it establishes in families into our understanding of Elvis. So let's say it clearly: He was an adult child of an alcoholic. As such, he was schooled in the patterns of conflict avoidance and dishonesty. Elvis most likely had an inherited genetic disposition for substance abuse. Gladys and he were certainly alike in their tendency to go to extremes in everything.

Let's also say this clearly. Gladys loved Elvis more than her own life. There is no doubt about that. But let's be honest. Elvis suffered from Gladys's enmeshment in his life. From the time of his birth, and particularly after Vernon's imprisonment, Gladys unfortunately, like many mothers, sought to live through her son. She unconsciously taught him to view himself as an extension of her ego. Obviously she was not deliberate about this, but for many, many years (possibly his entire life), Elvis never had a sense of his own identity. He never really felt that he had, within the boundaries of integrity, legitimate reasons to live his own life and make his own decisions. *He was brought up to find his fulfillment in pleasing others.* Not in *serving* them, but pleasing them. There is a difference. People who are motivated to please others rarely have their need to love and be loved met. Their lifelong search for that kind of fulfillment is often tragically unsuccessful.

Paradoxically, this extreme form of dependency on another person—and that person's problems—often manifests itself through a counterfeit heroism. Elvis became, at once, both Gladys's overly protected and pampered child, and, in his own mind, her emotional and physical support.

Again, I am not indicting Gladys. But over the past fifteen years the recovery movement has given us a very compassionate understanding of dysfunctional families. I loved my brother Elvis more than anyone else in the world while he was alive. My goal is not to condemn but to understand.

In Elvis's early reading he found an imaginative world with many parallels to his own feelings. He became intrigued by and almost obsessed with comic books, especially Captain Marvel, Jr. His interest in these comics tends to verify what may look like only cold and rather heartless theories. His later allusions to the comics show what a lasting hold they had on his imagination. More than thirty years later, in 1971, when the national organization of the Junior Chambers of Commerce gave him an award as one of its seven young men of the year, he said, commenting on his life, "I'd like you folks to know that I was the hero of the comic book. . . . So every dream that I ever dreamed has come true a hundred times." The insignia he gave to his touring crew, TCB (Taking Care of Business), included the same lightning bolt that Captain Marvel, Jr. wore on his chest as well.

Captain Marvel, Jr. appeared before his readers as "the most powerful boy in the world." (Not a bad description for Elvis in his later life.) This comic book hero led a double life. In everyday life, he appeared to others as the crippled boy, Freddy. Confronting an emergency situation, though, Freddy would name the magical wizard, "Shazam," and be transformed into the young hero.

Every child has such a fantasy life, of course, which is why the comic book appealed not only to Elvis but to millions of others as well. Every child feels crippled by his circumstances, if only the circumstances of his youth, lack of knowledge, and emotional maturity. Every child also has a magical facility, too, to transform himself into the most powerful child in the world; namely, imagination. Certainly, Elvis's peculiar circumstances intensified these identifications. He must have felt crippled by his father's prison record, his family's poverty, and his mother's need to be cared for. He desperately needed to be the most powerful boy in the world to shoulder the responsibility for the family that, however irrationally, he felt had fallen to him.

Plus, Elvis must have become aware as he grew up of how his family was regarded in the community. They were not only poor, they were considered as people from the wrong side of the tracks. Gladys's father could never adequately support his family. Her mother had several children, further complicating the family economic situation. Elvis's paternal great-grandmother, Rosella, bore ten children out of wedlock, including Vernon's father, Jesse. One of Vernon's sisters, Dixie, contracted syphilis through an adulterous affair and had to be institutionalized in a mental hospital at the end of her life. Elvis's paternal grandfather, Jesse, was an alcoholic. In fact, the family line has many alcoholics on both sides. Jesse eventually deserted Vernon's mother and ran off with another woman and started another family. Vernon was good-hearted and likable, but he would run afoul of the law again, when Elvis was thirteen, for making moonshine and distributing it, which caused the family to have to leave Tupelo. Skilled at carpentry, Vernon could have used this skill to earn a decent living, but for some reason he was never motivated sufficiently.

So Elvis assumed the mantle of family leadership, a role burdened by poverty, lack of social status, his mother's alcoholism, his father's prison record, and the simple fact that he was a child. What a burden. It's amazing that this young boy had the strength to handle these fully adult responsibilities. If any of his critics need a lesson in compassion, they don't need to look any further than Elvis's childhood to gain a respect for what he accomplished.

Later in life, an interviewer asked him, as he began to make his ascent to stardom, whether he should not put off his career, now that he had earned some money, and go to college. Elvis asked the questioner if he had ever been poor. That was enough of an answer for Elvis. I doubt the interviewer had any idea what Elvis meant by poor. Very few Americans can fully appreciate the poverty Elvis knew: a poverty of spirit even more desperate than his family's finances. He came from the dregs of society. Not from an oppressed minority, where at least a community solidarity alleviates the individual burden, he was only a poor relation of the ruling classes, the most marginalized of marginalized peoples. You see this and you think, Run away little boy. Get out of there any way you can. That life is going to kill you!

He did not run. Instead, as strange as this may be, he took up the family's burden and turned himself into their Captain Marvel, Jr. The odds of Elvis's making it were very slim, and any objective view of Elvis has to be made within this extraordinary context.

While not a blood relative of Elvis, I nevertheless learned many of the same dysfunctional patterns Elvis did while living with him for seventeen years. The major difference between us is that I wanted to live up to Elvis's glittering image, not live down my background. Sure, I enjoyed the material wealth that he brought into the lives of everyone around him, but I can tell you that a life lived only to please someone else—or even yourself—is sheer misery. When will the other person be pleased? When will you be pleased? When is it enough? What happens if someone suddenly changes the standards?

We were all wrapped up in this dysfunctional cycle of pleasing and peace making, with an underlying anger that had to be deadened before it would knock down the whole house of cards.

# 3

## Roots

*M*ost people think of Elvis as an overnight sensation: the truck driver who stopped off at a recording studio to record a song for his mother's birthday and found himself catapulted to fame. The male equivalent of Lana Turner at her drugstore counter on Hollywood and Vine. As I grew up as part of the Presley clan, I was certainly misled, like everyone else, by this image of Elvis as someone to whom everything came easily and almost unbidden.

Even Elvis read or misread his own story in this way. When asked by an interviewer early in his career whether he felt he was lucky or more talented than the next fellow, Elvis replied that he had been lucky. He came along at a time in the music business, he said, when no trend dominated. The music scene cried out for something new.

Elvis's public image very seldom stressed his talent, but he was given an enormous gift, which showed itself early, as musical talent almost always does. Mozart, after all, composed his first symphony at the age of six. He sat down at the piano and began to play almost flawlessly without any instruction whatsoever. Experts agree that a musician's potential usually shows itself by the age of sixteen.

As a child in the Tupelo Assembly of God church, Elvis ran up and down the aisles, moved to express the joy of the music in the only way that he could. His immersion in gospel music from that time was so great that later he claimed he knew "just about every religious song that had ever been written." Rock 'n' roll, he said, was mostly gospel, or gospel mixed with rhythm and blues. At one time he tried out for a gospel quartet. The Songfellows needed a baritone, and Elvis, at that point, sang tenor. He sang a lot of baritone during his mature career on his gospel albums, among the best, if not the best recordings, he ever produced. All his life he equated singing or hearing gospel with profound feelings of peace—like being in heaven, he said. For years I watched him sit down at the piano and chord out hymns to his own deeply resonant voice when he was troubled, needed to relax, or was searching for the inspiration to work at other types of music. It was his way, I think now, of experiencing God, his means of feeling God's love.

Gladys, Vernon, and Elvis sang trios in the First Assembly of God Church in East Tupelo and at camp meetings, revivals, and all-church sings. Elvis joined combinations of his many other relatives for special numbers. Those who still live in such Southern circles can better appreciate how casual and yet important this type of training can be. Almost anybody with a half-decent voice gets called upon to perform. Vernon had a good voice, and Gladys one that might have been developed professionally, as well as the feel for rhythm she demonstrated in her dancing. Elvis's family lived a life in which they went to church "every time the doors were open." As a little boy, Elvis heard the fervent, practiced singing of church people all around him. It was as much a part of his world as the smell of pine and honeysuckle. "When I was four or five," Elvis remembered, "all I looked forward to was Sundays, when we all could go to church. This was the only singing training I ever had."

Some people have been reluctant to acknowledge gospel music's influence on Elvis, both musically and spiritually. They like to think of him as the "hood," the teenage rebel, the hillbilly alley cat, Elvis the Pelvis, a bad boy of a highly erotic underworld. They have trouble thinking anything good can be connected with Pentecostalism, and they emphasize how much Elvis railed against uncompassionate preaching; how he spiritualized Christian doctrines in his searchings during the 1960s into an esoteric truth that was far more inclusive and tolerant than the faith of his childhood.

The themes of gospel music, though, more truly reflect Pentecostal teaching than the way Elvis characterized it at a certain time in his life. Elvis heard from Brother Gains Mansell and later from Brother Frank Smith—a preacher who stopped his sermons once in a while to sing and pluck a guitar he had strapped around his neck—of God's power and control over human destiny (as we hear in "How Great Thou Art"). He learned of God's compassion and care for his people, especially for the poor and downtrodden ("In the Garden"). The presence of God means peace in our lives ("Peace in the Valley"). He promises to protect us, guide us, and watch over us ("Peace in the Valley," "If the Lord Wasn't Walking by My Side"). The Lord is always there to enable us to meet life's problems ("Take My Hand, Precious Lord"). He is ready to assist us ("Where Could I Go But to the Lord"). He will be with us through this life and the next ("I'll Fly Away"). God is hardly pictured in gospel music or Pentecostalism as a cosmic bully.

An odd racism influences any discussion of Elvis's church and musical background. Some writers are willing to grant gospel music a measure of influence because many of the great gospel hymns were composed by blacks like the Reverend Thomas Dorsey. The gospel quartet style that influenced Elvis was based on pre-World War II black gospel styles, the "Dr. Watts" style, and the "jubilee." And the Reverend H. W. Brewster, an Afro-American, organized many of the all-night sings Elvis attended in Memphis. No one seems to question why it should be more palatable for Afro-Americans to express their Christian beliefs through music than Scotch-Irish Americans. The truth is that gospel music is a genuine folk art that belongs to the poor, to whites as well as blacks, although the mightiest rivers of gospel music come out of the black community. Elvis acknowledged that much of white psalm singing derives from Afro-American styles. It bears with it a message of love and protection for all the dispossessed. It represents a degree of cultural integration.

Elvis took steps, even as a child, to enjoy the full diversity of gospel music. He visited the black section of Tupelo, Shakerag, where he heard old men playing the blues on porches and gospel music, accompanied by guitar, piano, and tambourine, in the Sanctified Church. These incidents, like running up and down the church aisles as a toddler, show how Elvis's instinctive and powerful responses to music led him to behave in a way typical only of prodigies.

When Elvis was eight years old, he began performing on a local radio program, the "Saturday Jamboree" on WELO, which offered a chance at the mike to willing children. The host of the program, Charlie Boren, remembers Elvis singing there as often as every other Saturday. He performed gospel tunes, Gene Autry songs, and what became his old standby, Red Foley's "Old Shep," a sentimental song about a boy and his Lassie-like dog, that the boy has to put down himself in the tear-jerking end.

Elvis received his first guitar for his ninth or tenth birthday party. This famous story has several versions. The man who sold him the guitar, F. L. Bobo, says that when Gladys and Elvis first came into his store, Elvis wanted to buy a rifle. Others say that Elvis hoped for a bicycle. At any rate, Gladys steered Elvis in the direction of the guitar. Doing yard work for people, Elvis had saved a certain amount of money for his own birthday present, but he was short of the rifle's and the guitar's purchase prices. Gladys volunteered to make up the difference if Elvis would buy the guitar.

In the days afterward, Elvis had many guitar instructors, including Mississippi Slim, a professional country singer with his own program on WELO. Elvis got to know him by following him around like a pet dog. Mississippi Slim, or Carvel Lee Ausborn, had one of those whiny, reedy, yodeling country voices and the home-fried stage patter to match. He brought Elvis on to WELO's "Saturday Jamboree," and actually had him on his own program. Although he complained about the boy's inability to keep time, he said that Elvis was "doing a good job."

Elvis never became an accomplished guitarist, but he did learn to play the piano well, making whatever use he could of the

instruments at school and at church. He tau[...]
well enough to provide the accompaniment on[...]
ings, especially his gospel albums and his fam[...]
of "Unchained Melody." The piano, much m[...]
released his musical energies. I often saw him sit down at the piano at Graceland and sing alone or rouse those around him into
a jam session.

Once a year the Mississippi-Alabama Fair and Dairy Show
came to Tupelo, camping out about a half-mile from Elvis's
neighborhood. After a great deal of encouragement from
Gladys, Elvis entered the children's singing contest in 1945. The
ten-year-old boy stepped up to the microphone, strummed his
guitar for a measure or two as he began "Old Shep," and then
continued a cappella, too nervous to remember to play. His clear,
bewitching voice traveled out to the grandstand, which seated
two thousand people. However many there were in attendance
that day, they rewarded him with enough applause for him to
win second prize. He was given five dollars and free admission
to all the rides. Elvis was euphoric. The experience seems to
have confirmed his quiet determination to set his cap for a singing career. For the first time he experienced a type of love and
acceptance that the true performer can crave with an appetite
as desperate as any child looking for acceptance and approval.
Certainly, nothing would substitute for the emotional high Elvis
experienced in front of a crowd. When everything else that
made him happy was exhausted, he held tenaciously to the love
and acceptance of his fans, but that form of acceptance had its
limits too, unfortunately.

During the war years, Vernon and Gladys recouped their status in the community to a degree, and the war brought enough
work to the region for Vernon to make a better living. He worked
on a prisoner-of-war camp in nearby Como, Mississippi, and then
at a war plant in Memphis. The Presleys lost their house on Old
Saltillo Road through Vernon's first arrest, but then, after a bit of
wandering to Pascagoula and several rentals, they bought another
one from their old nemesis Orville Bean on Berry Street for the

ce of $2,000. Vernon even became a deacon at the First Assembly of God Church.

This might have been the happiest period in Gladys's life. There is good reason to believe that she coached Elvis in his singing and dreamed with him of a professional singing career. He performed any chance he got; he even sang outside the Tupelo Hotel on Spring Street for pocket change. Despite Gladys's overly protective nature, she gave him carte blanche to pursue any and all singing opportunities. She was not, as might be expected, a stage mother, sitting in on every WELO jamboree. She let him go alone across town to these shows and let him find his own rides.

A year after purchasing the house on Berry Street, though, the Presleys lost it, disastrously behind on their payments. Gladys could not control her impulsive buying habits. Vernon failed to find steady work.

After the family moved into an old shack on Mulberry Alley, Vernon found a job driving a truck for L. P. McCarty delivering wholesale goods, a job which he kept for almost three years. But this led to the family's being driven out of Tupelo after Vernon was caught hauling moonshine in the company truck.

So, in late September or early October (no one is sure of the exact date) 1948, the Presleys packed all their belongings into and on top of a 1939 Plymouth and headed for Memphis.

They soon moved into an old Victorian house that had been chopped into a number of apartments, and from there to Lauderdale Courts, an integrated housing project. Their apartment at Lauderdale Courts—two bedrooms, a kitchen, and a private bath—provided some of the best accommodations the Presleys had ever enjoyed. The government monitored their income, however, stipulating that they could not earn more than a given amount if they wished to stay. The Presleys resorted to cash-only jobs to improve their conditions, but they continually wavered between making too much money and getting too far behind in their rent. The jeers of Elvis's classmates at Humes High about where he was living seared his thoughts. He felt the stigma of the family's poverty keenly. He had been at home in

Tupelo even during the worst of times, but now, in Memphis, suffering from cruel jibes by his classmates, or the big city's blatant indifference to his family's and his own situation, he experienced a greater degree of alienation than he had ever known before. And this happened just at that time when an adolescent feels nearly paralyzed by the adult responsibilities lying in wait.

As Elvis began his teenage years, as he turned fourteen in Memphis, fifteen, then sixteen, he began to change his appearance, adopting his famous waterfall pompadour and d.a. haircut, growing sideburns, and buying flashy clothes. He went over to Lansky Brothers on Beale Street, the music district, and the secondhand shops that carried the same type of goods. These places catered to musicians, gamblers, and various shady characters. He liked the pants performers wore: pegged at the ankles, baggy at the knees, with pleated waists that rose up under the ribs, as high as a cummerbund. They often had insets along the seams, like tuxedo pants, only in neon colors. They wore skinny belts through the narrow loops of these pants, and fixed the clasp over at the side. Loud shirts completed these outfits, in polka dots or solid colors, banana yellows and turquoise. Later, in his twentieth year, he would discover his famous black and pink combinations. He started to wear his collars up like the musician "Mr. B." (Billy Eckstine) because he thought his neck was too long.

Although most parents find them embarrassing, the teenage wardrobes can be fascinating. They represent a language for what teenagers cannot say any other way, most often even to themselves. The message always declares something about the wearer's identity, or what they hope that identity will be. Elvis's transformation influenced so many others that its meaning for him tends to be obscured by what Elvis came to mean to the world.

The genius of Elvis's transformation lies in its paradoxical response to the pressures engulfing him. These pressures were very real. His mother looked to him to be her hero, but at the same time she made him act respectfully toward his father—an underachiever. In other words, at this most critical time of adolescence he was already shouldering much of the burden of adulthood. From the time, in fact, of his first yard jobs, Elvis worked constantly to support his family, delivering milk, working in the fields, helping the black grocers stock their goods and serve their customers.

Also, Elvis experienced what it was like to be a "work horse." He was dispossessed and scorned, among the poorest of the poor, looked down on by most in his home community, whose familiarity he then lost because of another family scandal. Sam Phillips said about him: "He felt so inferior."

So part of his transformation came about as a reactionary stance. You think I'm no good, he might have said to himself, well, I'll show how no-good I can be. This is a child's reaction to abuse. He will have the attention he craves, even if that attention comes in negative forms.

By moving with the pressures around him rather than against them, Elvis found another world, the world of music and entertaining in which his talents were highly valued. This world allowed him the benefit, too, of keeping one foot in the white community and the other in the black. He found out on Beale Street that being an honorary Afro-American had more than its share of compensations.

A lesser person would have simply resisted his neighbors' judgments of him and struggled upstream to little avail. An even more average person would simply have been defeated. But Elvis had the genius and somehow enough belief in himself to embrace his designated role and use it to his own advantage.

His hairstyle, sideburns, and clothing showed his identification with the underworld. He was angry about his position in society, and he had a right to be. But then, instead of channeling that anger into confrontation, instead of remaining simply the punk who will inevitably get his comeuppance, Elvis let the anger flower into a luxuriant and exotic aesthetic bloom—a new version of Tony Curtis, Marlon Brando, James Dean, and all his fellow rebels. They were rebels without a cause, but Elvis had a very real concern for getting himself and his family out of the projects!

Elaine Dundy remarked in *Elvis and Gladys* on how much Elvis's droopy forelock and ducktailed coif resembled Captain Marvel, Jr. In the end, the transformation, more than anything else, insisted that he still wanted to accomplish the epic task he accepted as a three-year-old. He wanted to take care of his family. He wanted to be its hero. He wanted the love and acceptance of his immediate family, and he had the touching notion that he could build up his family and enlarge his domain until it included the hostile outside world as well.

His physical transformation would have remained so much costuming, though, if he were not in the possession of a truly magical power: the ability to speak his heroic name, to sing it out, in fact, transforming himself through his art from Elvis Presley, an absolute nobody, into Elvis Presley, the king of rock 'n' roll. Just like in the comic books, as he said, he was then able to transform his world, and, to a stunning degree, ours, too.

You have to be incredibly mean-spirited not to love the guy. He could not have said these things about his transformation, of course. If he had been able to spell it out in so many words, he would not have needed so much the symbols of the transformation itself. Its importance to him, though, cannot be doubted, because he risked life and limb every time he went to Humes High School looking like that. His nearly lifelong friend, Red West, had to rescue him once from a group who had ganged up on him in a bathroom and were threatening to cut his hair. He left the football team when he was told he could not make the squad without getting a haircut. And he kept to his own style even when he joined the ROTC.

What appears to be his only moment of acceptance in high school came with the variety show staged in his senior year. Thirty acts entered the competition. Elvis, after borrowing a solid red shirt from his friend Buzzy Forbes, sang "Cold, Cold, Icy Fingers" and his standard, "Old Shep." The audience's applause awarded him first place. When he came off the stage after his encore, he was congratulated by his homeroom teacher, Miss Scrivener, who had encouraged him to enter the competition. "They really like me, Miss Scrivener. They really like me!" he blurted out.

That is what he wanted most of all, to be loved. The true hall-marks of his growing-up years occur on those few occasions when he performs and stuns the crowd. They confirmed him in his dreams, and gave him a taste of the fame he came to crave.

After graduation, he hitchhiked to Meridian, Mississippi, and the first Jimmie Rodgers "Father of Country Music" Festival. He won second place and a new guitar.

After doing some factory work, Elvis took a job driving a truck for Crown Electric. This allowed him to be out and about during the day without someone looking over his shoulder, paid him enough to keep himself and heavily subsidize the family income, and left his nights free for visiting clubs around town, especially on Beale Street, and performing on a spot basis. He appeared at dives like Hernando's Hideaway and The Eagle's Nest. He dodged some beer bottles and began to learn what worked and what didn't.

Just after his eighteenth birthday, when the Presleys were once again being hassled by the Lauderdale Courts housing authority, Elvis insisted his family move into private housing. There seems good reason to believe that Elvis met Bill (Blackie) Black, the bass player in his original recording combo, while still at Lauderdale Courts. Although for years the story has been told that Sam Phillips, the owner of Sun Records, introduced Elvis to Bill Black and Scotty Moore, Blackie's mother, Ruby, lived at Lauderdale Courts, and Blackie's son insists that he heard Elvis, Bill, and Scotty jamming together there years before Elvis met Sam Phillips. Everyone agrees that Elvis used to serenade his neighbors in the projects, and it would hardly have been out of the ordinary for good musicians to hook up.

It seems that Blackie encouraged Elvis to make use of the recording service at Sun Studios. Anyone could make an acetate record there for only four dollars.

The first time Elvis went in on a Saturday. He met Sam Phillip's right-hand woman, Marion Keisker. She was managing the place that day. She asked him who he sounded like.

"I don't sound like nobody," he said.

She asked him if he sang hillbilly songs. He said he did. "Who do you sound like in hillbilly?"

"I don't sound like nobody," he said again.

Elvis sang two Ink Spot tunes, "My Happiness" and "That's When Your Heartaches Begin." Before the end of the first song, Marion had threaded the alternate machine and made a duplicate recording of the end of the first number and all of the second. She made a note, "Good ballad singer." She asked Elvis for his address and phone number. The Presleys did not have their own phone, but the rabbi who lived below them sometimes took messages for them. Marion's request for the information obviously meant she had been impressed. She told Elvis they might be calling.

Marion remembered Sam saying over and over again, "If I could find a white man who had the Negro sound and the Negro feel, I could make a billion dollars." Marion immediately heard and sensed that Elvis had "soul."

Elvis went home with his record and exciting news. He had told Marion that he was making the recording for his mother's birthday, which was, in fact, long since past. But his statement had a lot of poetic truth to it. Everything he did to further his career, he did equally for himself and his mother. Gladys was, of course, overjoyed at his new prospects.

Although Marion conveyed her favorable impressions to Sam Phillips, he did nothing about it. Blackie kept encouraging Elvis to go in and make another record. Sam was recording more white country-western singers now.

In January 1954, Elvis showed up again to make another record. This time Sam Phillips himself was in the control booth. Elvis recorded "Casual Love Affair" and a country song, "I'll Never Stand in Your Way." Phillips was impressed enough to follow in Marion Keisker's footsteps, making a note of the singer's address and the phone at which he could be reached.

Sometime after that, when a demo tape came in of a ballad, "Without You," by an unknown singer, Sam Phillips did not know exactly what to do. He liked the song enough to put out a record, but he could not find a singer. This time he remembered the "good ballad singer."

Sam telephoned Elvis. He used to say that the boy arrived almost before Sam had hung up the phone.

Elvis's first recording session at Sun, as he tried to mimic the singer's voice on "Without You," went badly. Elvis found his inability to nail the song so frustrating that he lost control of his emotions. He threw a temper tantrum, striking out at the air and railing against his invisible rival.

During a break, Phillips asked Elvis what he could sing.

"I can sing anything," Elvis said, quickly reversing field.

"Do it," Sam ordered.

So he did. Elvis went through the complete catalog of songs he had ever memorized, some of them he had only half-memorized, some he simply knew in snatches. He did a lot of Dean Martin crooning, but he also sang the blues and went through the songs he performed in places like Hernando's Hideaway and The Eagle's Nest—honky-tonk jump music, old standards, and, of course, gospel. The boy who knew "every religious song that's ever been written," had perfect pitch, was a gifted mimic, and could usually pick up any tune by ear after two or three run-throughs started to display his already powerful life in music.

Sam began to recognize, finally, the dimensions of his talent. He recognized that Elvis had no set style and was *too* given to brilliant imitation. Like a young thoroughbred horse, he needed work to run and find his own gait.

Sam arranged for Elvis to rehearse with the guitar player, Scotty Moore, and the standup bass player, Bill Black. Elvis most probably already knew these men. They were part of a band called The Starlite Wranglers, and surely, even if Blackie's son's memory is inaccurate, Elvis had seen them perform out on the country-western circuit.

Scotty, Blackie, and Elvis started working out their sound in the studio, benefiting from a chance to find their music away from critical audiences and with the advantage of many takes and playbacks. They all played by ear, and the new sound they arrived at might never have been possible in another era, one without the benefits of electronic trial-and-error. Soon enough, they found "That's All Right Mama."

Elvis changed the rules of the game. He took the status game and enlarged the playing field to include the integrated world of music. He ended up scoring in more ways and more often than anyone in his schools in Tupelo or at Humes High ever suspected. But the thought still comes to me that for all of his genius, he was still playing the game. He used his musicianship to gain an unprecedented measure of power. That power brought with it the adoration of countless fans and millions of dollars. Was that, though, what he was really after? The role he made up, the starring role, in the new rock 'n' roll game, remained, to its author, a fiction. He knew that the Elvis the public would soon know and the Tupelo boy inside differed. As Elvis said, an image is a hard thing to live up to. What if he had never played at all—his game or anyone else's? Was that an option? The way he transcended his situation required a sense of genius, but I wonder if that was the transcendence he truly wanted or only a counterfeit image of something much better.

# 4

## The Miracle Year

*D*ewey Phillips, a disc jockey at WHBQ in Memphis, aired "That's All Right" on his "Red, Hot, and Blue" radio show on Wednesday, July 7, 1954. He always took requests and talked with his listeners. That night his incoming call board lit up like a Christmas tree. Everyone wanted to hear the song again. He played "That's All Right" and its flipside, "Blue Moon of Kentucky," over and over again.

Phillips normally played only music by black recording artists, or "race music" as it was then called. He wanted Elvis to come on his program that night so that his listeners could hear Elvis himself say that he had attended the segregated Humes High and to verify that the singer was white.

Elvis had gone to the movies, knowing his record would be played that night. He tuned in his radio at home to the station, instructing his parents to leave it there, before going out. They heard his name, Elvis Presley, being repeated again and again as the disc jockey kept playing his record. They took the call and found Elvis at the theater, telling him that a lot was happening— all good.

Elvis went on Dewey Phillips's show and became a local celebrity. Music stores received five thousand orders for the record in the next week, before it had even been pressed.

Scotty Moore and Bill Black dropped out of their country-western band, The Starlite Wranglers, and began to tour with

Elvis. They barnstormed through Tennessee, Louisiana, Mississippi, and Texas as The Blue Moon Boys, with Elvis featured as "The Hillbilly Cat." After "That's All Right," Sun Records released "Good Rockin' Tonight" and "I Don't Care If the Sun Don't Shine," and then his third single in January 1955, "Milkcow Blues Boogie" and "You're a Heartbreaker." The second and third singles rocked even harder than the first and confounded radio programmers; Elvis was too country for some, too "race" for others.

Elvis did receive national radio exposure on an ill-fated visit to the "Grand Ole Opry" program (the manager suggested he return to truck driving) and became a regular on "The Louisiana Hayride," which meant commuting to Shreveport every weekend. Within six months of his first single's release, he quit his job at Crown Electric and began singing full time. The next two singles did poorer than the first, though, and Elvis's career threatened, he thought, to stall out.

The next record, "Baby Let's Play House" and its flipside, "I'm Left, You're Right, She's Gone," climbed the local charts in the areas where the band had toured—Houston, New Orleans, Nashville, Dallas, and Richmond. Its guitarist, Scotty Moore, handled bookings for the band at first. Then Sam Phillips suggested Elvis let another local disc jockey and club owner, Bob Neal, manage the band. He landed the "Hayride" gig and then arranged for Elvis to tour with country star Hank Snow.

On May 1, 1955, the Hank Snow tour began, crisscrossing Louisiana, Alabama, and northern Florida. Elvis and his band started out on the first half of the bill with other beginning acts, including Hank Snow's son, Jimmie Rodgers Snow, and the Davis Sisters and the Wilburn Brothers. They quickly learned that these performers couldn't follow Elvis. He was moved to the slot before intermission and then to the second half of the show, with the headliners—the Carter family, Slim Whitman, and the boss, Hank Snow, himself.

Elvis gave a scorching performance at the Gator Bowl in Jacksonville, Florida on May 13. He stuttered and shuddered and wiggled and writhed. He appeared in a pink suit, with a lacy, see-through shirt. The girls had already started screaming and rushing the stage in those days, and on this night Elvis had the women in the audience yearning for him with a violent passion. He ended the show by shouting out, "Thank you ladies and gentlemen." Then, in a devilish stage whisper, he breathed into the microphone, "Girls—I'll see you backstage."

Half the audience took him up on the invitation, cornering Elvis in a locker room. They tore at his clothes and threatened to tear him apart. He climbed on top of a shower stall to escape the frenzy, and the police finally cleared the room.

When he came out that evening into the parking lot, he found his new pink Cadillac had become a graffiti billboard of women's names and phone numbers, some painted on with lipstick and others scratched into the paint with pins and rings.

At that point, Colonel Thomas Andrew Parker, Hank Snow's manager and the owner of the agency booking the tour, became convinced he should start managing Elvis. Bob Neal might well have seen the evening in Jacksonville as horrifying and inexplicable; Colonel Parker saw a business opportunity. A performer capable of inspiring such passion had an uncommon future.

As part of Elvis's family, and later as a member of his working crew, I believed, like everyone around me, that Elvis would never have gotten where he did without his famous manager, Colonel Tom Parker. The Colonel had a hold on everyone around him, including me. I've seen members of Elvis's touring crew, tough guys like Red and Sonny West, get down on their knees and pretend to be dogs for the amusement of the Colonel's business associates. Elvis himself often fumed about the Colonel's decisions and hated his compulsive gambling. He literally dropped millions of dollars at the roulette wheel in Las Vegas. But Elvis never broke his ties with the Colonel, and those ties became stronger and more manaclelike through the years. At the end of Elvis's career, the Colonel's hold on Elvis was like the tethering of a trained elephant. A mature elephant can break away from almost any physical restraint. But if you take a baby elephant and restrain it successfully, when it matures, that elephant can be kept in its place by the most mediocre knot. It's conditioned to believe it cannot move, and so it doesn't. And the Colonel had us all conditioned—or brainwashed.

As I've pieced together my thoughts about Elvis over the years, though, an experience came back to me that gave me a different perspective on the Colonel. As a young evangelist I was visiting with him immediately following Vernon Presley's funeral in 1979. This was two years after Elvis's death. The Colonel had grown suddenly older, slowed by heart problems. A stroke had made one side of his face look slack, the eyelid lazy over one eye, the corner of his mouth on that side twisting down. Still smoking one of his stogies, he looked sadly pathetic.

When I told him of the crowds coming to my meetings, though, his eyes sharpened and a grin tightened up his sagging mouth. The old ball-bearing hardness returned to his light, bouncy blue eyes. "Listen," he said, "I've heard about your work with kids. I could do with you what I did with Elvis. Make you as big in your line of work as Elvis was in his. I could have you speaking in packed-out stadiums and coliseums."

I really believed he could do it. I felt like I'd been taken up on an exceedingly high mountain and shown all the kingdoms of the world and their glory and been made the devil's offer of fame and power.

Since the devil, in this case, looked like an old man, the offer could hardly be taken seriously, and that made it easy to turn down. I turned to the Colonel and said, "Colonel, I fear the Lord." But I understood better what Elvis felt when the Colonel made his pitch to him. "Right now, son," the Colonel is reported to have said, "you are *worth* a million dollars. If you go with me, you'll *have* the million."

Colonel Parker might not be the devil himself, but he is certainly as enticing, by his own design, as a real one. While I don't want to be harsh or judgmental about him, there are abundant resources available that give an accurate portrait of the man, and so I feel compelled to be true to the record. In 1957, about a year after taking over Elvis's career, the Colonel gave an interview to a reporter in which he claimed to be born in Huntington, West Virginia, on June 26, 1909. He said that his parents died before he turned ten years old, so he hit the road for the first time with his uncle's Great Parker Pony Circus.

When he left his uncle's troupe at seventeen, he struck out on his own with a pony-and-monkey act on the "cherry soda circuit," a small-time carnival tour where the acts, under contract to a soft drink maker, accepted bottle tops as the price of admission.

Then Parker said he became a press agent for a number of carnivals, circuses, and showboats. He married his wife, Marie, in 1932 while wintering with a carnival in Tampa, Florida.

From independent sources, we know that the Colonel served in the army in 1930–31. Then he worked for Royal American Shows, the first traveling carnival to take big-city scale amusement rides from stop to stop. Parker seems to have performed a variety of jobs for the Royal American Shows, including barker, cashier, commissary head, press agent, and maybe even psychic reader. His whole sense of promotion came from carnivals. He believed in massive and unremitting promotion. Posters everywhere. Blanket radio announcements. Handbills dropped from helicopters. Enough publicity to make anyone positively beg to purchase whatever the product happened to be. He also believed fervently in the P. T. Barnum philosophy encapsulated in the famous circus man's two statements: A sucker is born every minute, and never give a sucker an even break. All his life, Parker not only wanted to make money, but make money giving the customer as little as possible. He delighted in such scams as painting sparrows yellow and selling them as canaries. Strewing the ground outside of carnival tents with manure so he could sell pony rides to those fastidious of their shoes. He put on an exhibit of chickens "dancing" on a hot plate to the tune of "Turkey in the Straw."

He became a dog catcher in Tampa in 1940, where he transformed the back of the pound into a "pet cemetery." He sold funeral packages, which included day-end throwaways from florists. He also positioned an animal aid relief barrel in the pound's foyer, Parker apparently was the one who enjoyed the contributions.

He started managing the country singer, Gene Austin, during the war years. Austin is best known for the standard, "My Blue Heaven," the bestseller of all time until Bing Crosby's "White Christmas."

In 1945, Colonel Parker hooked up with another country singer, Eddy Arnold, and built him into a major star, a "Grand Ole Opry" regular and a recording artist for RCA. His own man, Arnold eventually tired of Colonel Parker's intrusive management style—Parker and his wife moved in with him for frighteningly long "visits" in Arnold's Madison, Tennessee home—and fired him in 1953.

His loss of Arnold as a client must have sent shockwaves through Colonel Parker's system. Although full of bluster, ballyhoo, and bunk, he was a more insecure man than he appeared to be, and with good reason. Enough spade work has been done to report, with as much reliability as Parker's secrecy allows, that Colonel Parker was actually born Andreas Cornelius van Kuijk in Breda, Holland on his acknowledged date of birth. He seems to have taken passage on a tramp steamer, jumped ship, and entered the country illegally. He probably joined the army, among other reasons, to establish a paper trail that would support his claims of being American-born. But he never filed for a passport, not even when Elvis went into the army and was stationed in Germany. A *very* strange nonevent in the life of a manager constantly in a sweat to maintain his control over his client. He overpaid his taxes. And in a business as litigious as the music and movie-making industries, he managed never to sue or be sued. All in all, it paints a portrait of someone who wants as little to do with the government as possible.

The Gator Bowl show convinced Parker that Elvis might well be the world's greatest sideshow (if not the world's greatest entertainer)—a hillbilly who inspired a mythic devotion and passion of his own.

With Elvis's being under age at the time, Parker had to woo Vernon and Gladys in his quest to take over Elvis's management from Bob Neal. He pursued his objective on his own, dangling dollar signs in front of Vernon's eyes. Through emissaries like the comic Whitey Ford and the headliner Hank Snow, men whose beliefs and manners matched the Presleys, the Colonel worked on Gladys.

The Colonel brought real assets to the table that everyone had to acknowledge. Through his association with Eddy Arnold, he had good contacts with the "Grand Ole Opry," RCA, and premiere singing venues around the country. Bob Neal saw this, and although he disagreed with Parker's decisions, like getting Elvis out of his contract with the "Louisiana Hayride," his reservations were conquered by greed. Parker cut Bob Neal into the new deals he arranged for Elvis as a "consultant," deals that upped Neal's percentage of the take substantially—but only for a time. Parker cut Neal in so he could cut him out. Parker's deals with Neal, unlike his deals with Elvis, had termination dates.

Similarly, the first agreement Elvis signed with Parker called for Parker to act as a consultant in partnership with Hank Snow. Parker and Snow both felt that Elvis needed a bigger record label than Sun. They discussed how to buy him out of his Sun contract in order to sell him to another label. Parker suggested that Hank Snow put up *all* of his RCA royalties. Naturally, this was unacceptable to Snow. Parker knew it would be, but deliberately misread Snow's refusal to mean he no longer considered himself a partner to Elvis's management. Without further ado, Parker arranged for RCA to buy out Elvis's contract with Sun, with additional financing provided by the music publisher Hill and Range. He did get the astronomical price, for the time, of thirty-five thousand dollars. Five thousand went directly into Elvis's pocket, and that overcame Elvis's own doubts about leaving Sam Phillips and Bob Neal and casting his lot with the wheeling and dealing Parker.

The destructive seeds of much of Elvis's later troubles lay in this arrangement, however. Parker thought of his "boy"—the most derisive imaginable term in a Southerner's mouth—as just another show, a come-on for the suckers, a commodity. When Elvis died, he thought that nothing would change. He knew that there would still be ways to package and sell Elvis. For him, nothing had changed. For those of us who loved Elvis, of course, everything had changed. Our whole world had been tragically changed.

In the same way, he cared very little for Elvis's music; he often made sarcastic comments about Elvis's act, once volunteering that if Elvis didn't sing, he could just get up on the stage and wiggle. He was, in fact, the one who encouraged Elvis to become more conscious of his mannerisms, and delighted in transforming him into something more provocative.

At the time Elvis signed with the Colonel, he was still very naive and uninformed. Having grown up in poverty and felt stigmatized further by his first home community and rendered anonymous by the next, Elvis wanted nothing so much as he wanted *out!* Parker presented what appeared his most lively hope.

The Colonel also must have looked to Elvis like an appropriate father figure, the kind of guide his life had conspicuously lacked. How many young men go through their twenties adopting older colleagues, bosses, or their in-laws as substitute fathers? We even encourage "re-parenting" and "mentoring relationships" now, even though the person needs to give up on the perfect father dream, accept his rearing for what it has been, and go on. Still, such a desire on Elvis's part might well be expected. Inexperienced as he was, he must have been easy prey to Parker, mistaking the older man's veneer of prestige and bluster for authority and power.

The Colonel encouraged this view of himself at every turn. He rattled off the complicated terms of business arrangements to Elvis, deliberately confusing him to deepen his dependence. He constantly impressed on Elvis, and all who would listen, that the Colonel's boy would be nothing without him. The stories he gave to the press, like the interview he granted *Time* magazine in 1962, established this notion in the public's mind as well. He restrained him from making any of his own decisions early on. Later, when

Elvis had matured, he still felt conditioned by this schooling in dependence. The Colonel was given to blackmailing his associates, and God only knows what he told Elvis, what he held over his head. There have also been stories about the Colonel threatening to reveal Vernon's criminal record. He may have done these things; he may not have. He certainly did bring whatever pressures he could in teaching Elvis the lessons of psychological dependence. He did not want a repeat of his summary dismissal by Eddy Arnold. He taught Elvis from his earliest associations with him that he could not get away, and when Elvis had finally matured, for whatever reasons, he still believed this devastating lie.

To give the Colonel his due, though, the first full year Elvis spent under the his management must go down in the history of the entertainment business as Elvis's own miracle year, his *annum mirabile.*

Two days after Elvis turned twenty-one, on January 10 and 11, 1956, Elvis recorded in RCA's Nashville studios. Steve Sholes produced the sessions. Chet Atkins, a star in his own right, an outstanding guitarist with a pure, melodic style, assisted in the production and played second guitar. D. J. Fontana, who now toured with Elvis, played the drums. Floyd Cramer filled out the group's sound on piano, and the Jordanaires, a gospel trio, sang back up.

Elvis recorded the song that perhaps more than any other made him a phenomenon: "Heartbreak Hotel." He wails out the first two lines, "Well, since my baby left me / I've found a new place to dwell," and then his voice lends a subtle syncopation to the next line with a subdued bop to each step—"it's down at the end of Lonely Street." Blackie's standup bass, sounding like a one-string instrument reverberating in a washer tub, follows the line down, trailing the singer's bluesy steps. "It's called Heartbreak Hotel." We arrive together with our broken hearts at a common destination.

But then, Elvis seems to address the listener instead of the girl who has left him, putting all his heart-wrenching soul into one line and popping his voice and those bee-stung lips on *"baa-buh."*

"I get so lonely, ba-buh / I get so l-lonely / I get so lonely / I could die." The line wasn't far removed from his Gator Bowl whisper, "See you backstage—girls." Who wouldn't want to comfort a brokenhearted young idol? Almost every woman in the country did after hearing that soulful voice.

In this session Elvis also recorded "Money Honey" and "I Got a Woman." He sounds more bluesy than ever in this last song, and it's one of his best.

On January 28, 1956, Elvis went on television, "The Dorsey Brothers Stage Show." The Dorsey Brothers' ratings were weak, and so they were willing to take a chance on a young talent who might lend the show some vitality. Watching the tapes of the old show, you see why. They had a Busby Berkeley chorus line (Jackie Gleason produced the show, and he always kept the June Taylor Dancers on hand, even into the 1960s). The male acts were sedate, dressed in tuxedos. Elvis appears in the midst of this with the impact of a gunshot going off in a movie theater. He brought some vitality to the show, all right.

From the moment he starts singing "Heartbreak Hotel," he is in control of himself and his audience. He knew immediately how to play to both the camera and the audience; to bring each member of the audience into his performance so that he seems to sing to each of them individually. When you see the tapes now of The Beatles performing on Ed Sullivan or in concert, you see that the music itself conditioned most of the fans' reaction. Elvis's television performances themselves are still highly affecting, emotionally charged. His personal magnetism is timeless.

"Heartbreak Hotel" soon topped the national pop and country charts. Elvis and his band continued to tour through the South and Southwest, with occasional jaunts into the Midwest. They were hitting bigger venues now, arenas as well as theaters and auditoriums. The groundswell of fan adoration was just building, though. Television would continue to play a key role.

On April 23, Elvis and his band appeared as headliners at the Frontier Hotel in Las Vegas. This date went badly. Las Vegas has always been, and continues to be, a middle-aged mecca. When you arrive in Sin City, you find the sinners are mostly paunchy, wattled, gray, and double-knitted or polyesterized (whatever the bad fabric of the moment happens to be). It's a shock. Initially, the crowds turned out in Las Vegas to gawk at Elvis, the hillbilly phenomenon. But he couldn't get his message across. He represented something fresher than the usual blue humor at Vegas, wilder than government-approved-and-taxed wagering.

Cruising the strip, Elvis and his band heard Freddie Bell and the Bellboys do a jumping version of Big Mama Thornton's 1953 R&B hit, "Hound Dog." They added "Hound Dog" to the act.

The second time Elvis went on "The Milton Berle Show," he performed "Hound Dog," his voice gritty with protest, the drums behind him exploding with the pumping energy that sent him into his ecstatic, head-shaking, knee-swiveling, leg-quaking dance. This performance of "Hound Dog" brought to a head the various protests against Elvis's style that had already been lodged. Critics decried his music as vulgar. They called him Elvis the Pelvis, a phrase the singer said was "the most childish expression I've ever heard comin' from an adult."

The music business itself had not received Elvis with open arms. Many adopted the attitude of the manager at the Grand Ole Opry. *Billboard* magazine received outraged protests against listing Elvis's music on the country-western charts. Citizens committees were organized to protest Elvis's show. Elvis expressed his befuddlement. "I can't figure it out," he said, "I mean, how would rock 'n' roll music make anybody rebel against their parents?"

Actually, looking at this now, more was at stake here for the country and for Elvis personally than most of us realize. Elvis and the vital forces he represented won handily. And the victors write the history books. The commentators on the side of the victors have so denounced the defenders of decency that objected to Elvis that we tend to overlook the impact of these protests on everything, including Elvis's career and his own personal destiny.

At the very beginning, Elvis moved instinctively to his music. He genuinely did not mean to be provocative, but the Colonel saw, though, that many of Elvis's movements were very suggestive. So he encouraged Elvis to refine his most provocative moves and invent others.

The question of what kind of sexual appeals should be made in entertainment is a legitimate one. Those who protested against Elvis in 1956 seemed to believe, though, that sexuality can be conveniently separated from other human actions. Any public performance, even a political speech, tends to deliver a healthy dose of highly charged emotion with it, which is why politicians have so many opportunities to betray their trusts. All dramatic actions arouse our passions and *ought* to. They excite us and provide a harmless outlet of natural and healthy feelings. But there is a line. When entertainment becomes inappropriately sensuous, whether in performance or on paper, it excites passion in such an inappropriate way that the audience can *act* on these passions.

I think it was totally acceptable for Elvis to be an emotional singer with sex appeal. He appealed to the passions of his audience and provoked them, but he also pulled back from them. People did not have to take his entreaties seriously, and a lot of what he did deliberately put them off. His manner conveyed the message: We are having fun—this is play acting. It is easier for us to see this today than it was for the citizens committees in 1956. America was so uptight at that time, though, that the nation needed an Elvis Presley. Badly. Perry Como, Frank Sinatra, and Bing Crosby would never do in the long run. Victorian prudishness is far less attractive than the sometimes bawdy realism of a more rowdy age. Both attitudes are possible to cultures formed by Christian values.

Saying this, Elvis sometimes went over the line. He gave himself moral holidays, screening that area off from his other beliefs and adopting at different times the double standard of male chauvinism.

As the controversy raged, Elvis appeared on "The Steve Allen Show." Allen hated rock 'n' roll, finding it barbarous. He set out to embarrass Elvis the best he could. He dressed Elvis in a tuxedo and blue suede shoes and then sent him out to sing "I Want You, I Need You, I Love You." The tux did not work badly with this slow ballad.

Next Allen had Elvis sing "Hound Dog" to a basset hound, who wore a top hat and tie himself. You can see Elvis swallowing, preparing himself for the ordeal. Still, he fawns over and makes up to the dog with such good humor that the audience's sympathies are definitely with the singer (and the dog who has to endure the television lights).

Finally, Allen introduced Elvis into a hayseed comedy sketch and song with Imogene Coca, Andy Griffith, and himself. The hayseed jokes and the song are such a lame parody, Elvis so obviously good-natured about the fiasco, that Allen's ploys totally backfire. Maybe he only meant to show that Elvis was just another performer, nothing special. If so, Elvis's genuine humility and childhood training to respect his elders helped him turn this entirely to his own advantage. He comes off as a trouper. His talents shine even in these derisive formats.

The Allen show pointed out something else that was wrong about Elvis's critics. Their motivations were not so much moral as they were cultural. Steve Allen, a New York sophisticate, did not like American culture being returned to its roots in the figure of Elvis Presley. He preferred a European gloss. That's not what's unique to the American experience, though. The contribution America has to make to world culture follows the route traveled by Mark Twain and Huck Finn, blues and gospel, not the New York crowd and its European borrowings.

Elvis appeared three times on "The Ed Sullivan Show." At first Ed Sullivan was as reluctant to let Elvis on his stage as Steve Allen was, but he relented when Elvis's Dorsey and Berle appearances made him the hottest ticket in show business. Sullivan, although his cameras shot Elvis only from the waist up on his last appearance, came out at the end of the final show (at the Colonel's insistence) and told the nation what a "decent, fine boy" Elvis was. This cooled some of the controversy.

Still, the cultural defenders missed how Elvis's music united two genuinely American styles—gospel and the blues. They pigeonholed Elvis as a crude hillbilly and wanted to write him off. But his popularity saved him. So the establishment accepted him, if reluctantly, as a money-making machine, betraying their own lack of genuine standards.

Elvis, for his part, saw his worst nightmare realized. He was again stigmatized by his impoverished upbringing. He could make all the money he wanted, but in the eyes of the establishment he thought he would never be anything more than an unsophisticated flash in the pan.

How he must have resented this. Behind the polite facade—a facade of manners being the traditional refuge of the oppressed—Elvis must have been seething.

Anger rarely makes us smart, though, except in attacking our enemies. Often it makes us accept the very standards by which we have been falsely judged. We dispute whether our enemies are right in their judgments rather than questioning the whole framework of their thinking. This is in part what happened with Elvis. You think I'm only good for commercial purposes, he seemed to be saying, Well, fine, I'll make more money than you've ever seen. I don't need you.

He did not need them, but he needed something more than the commercial standards he accepted. He needed to value his talent, the source for all the money. I'm not sure he ever managed this—not to the extent he should have, at any rate.

Elvis signed a three-picture, nonexclusive contract with the producer Hal Wallis in April. He took a screen test in August, playing a teenager rebelling against his no-account father, a role he understood only too well.

For his first movie, Wallis loaned Elvis out to Fox Studios. He was cast in a western originally entitled *The Reno Brothers*. The producers retitled the film *Love Me Tender* to take advantage of their young star's hit record. The story concerned two brothers who were in love with the same woman—played by Debra Paget—with fratricidal consequences. Elvis performed creditably enough, particularly since he was not given any coaching.

Elvis made three films over the next eighteen months. *Loving You, Jailhouse Rock,* and *King Creole* were shot in quick succession. Elvis had a natural screen presence. He could have developed into the kind of actor who essentially plays himself, while adjusting his emotional range to the dimensions of the part, like Gary Cooper, Cary Grant, or Jimmy Stewart. His scripts, though, called for him to play himself all too literally. They were versions of his life story, which often presented him in a demeaning context. What if Cary Grant were called on to repeatedly play a Britisher who started out as a vaudeville acrobat and eventually became an international star? Grant's true story might have made for an interesting story once, but afterward it would have proven tiresome, despite Grant's tremendous charm. Elvis played variations on the theme of his own life in 90 percent of his thirty-three films. At the end, in what Elvis himself called his "travelogues," he was doing little more than singing mostly mediocre material in exotic locations.

The intentions of the scripts often paralleled Steve Allen's. The stories usually showed a rock 'n' roller, a young punk, or a callow youth still wet behind the ears who needed to be taken under somebody's wing, usually an older woman's, and integrated into society. Elvis, as the hero, got the girl, and society was enabled to remain complacent in its materialistic values.

What if, for once, Elvis had been presented as an outsider, a second-class citizen? Someone who challenged the Eastern establishment and middle American philistinism alike, who changed the status game according to his own rules and won? Now that would have been interesting. At least once.

The Colonel cared very little for the intrinsic value of these films. He saw them as a convenient way to present his "boy" to the largest possible audience at staggered intervals. He concerned himself with the spinoff possibilities, the soundtrack albums and his line of Elvis merchandise. In 1956, the American public could purchase necklaces, phonographs, mittens, bracelets, shoes, stuffed hound dogs, pen-pal magazines, toreador pants, Bermuda shorts, ballpoint pens, dolls, buttons, colognes, soda pop, bubblegum cards, board games, pajamas, belts, glow-in-the-dark autographed pictures, and guitars with Elvis's name on them.

The Colonel, in fact, seemed to make every effort to isolate Elvis. He did not want him to start thinking of himself as a talented performer within a group of peers. When Elvis went to Hollywood, he started hanging around with that generation's brat pack: Sal Mineo, Dennis Hopper, Nick Adams, Russ Tamblyn, and Elvis's new love, Natalie Wood. These people might have taught Elvis that the going rate for management was 10 to 15 percent, not the 25 percent (and eventually 50 percent) that Colonel Parker charged. Even more, they would have helped Elvis gain the confidence he needed to start making his own decisions. To see that his manager sometimes acted in his own best interests, rather than his client's. The Colonel wanted to keep Elvis dumb, dependent, and emotionally fixated in adolescence. It's a lot easier to manipulate a child than an adult.

The Colonel received credit as the technical adviser of Elvis's pictures. Normally, this attribution describes someone who helps the producers with historical, technological, or cultural detail. A real, live Minnesota Fats, for example, on a picture about hustling in pool halls. The Colonel seems to have introduced a number of menacing jokes into the plot lines of Elvis's films. Is it a coincidence that Elvis's role in *Jailhouse Rock* combines Vernon's criminal record with Elvis's ascent to stardom? The Colonel's own wish-fulfillment fantasy seems to be introduced in *Jailhouse* when Elvis's alter ego, Vince Everett, who is being swindled without his knowing it, thanks his manager for only taking 50 percent of his earnings. The Colonel would not be able to make this prophetic dream come true in real life for more than a decade. Some commentators have remarked on how Elvis's demeanor changed on the set of *Jailhouse Rock*. He seems to have taken offense at the Colonel's "technical advice," seeing it as blackmail.

Elvis toured frantically during the first nine months of the year. Highlights included his triumphant return to the Mississippi-Alabama Fair. Tupelo declared "Elvis Presley Day." Elvis signed his check back over to the city, the first of many contributions he made to a children's recreation center close by his old neighborhood "above the highway" as well as other charities.

Elvis still ran into citizens committees. In Jacksonville, Florida, the authorities warned him that he was not to engage in the gyrations that had caused a riot the year before. Elvis went on stage, and instead of his usual swivels, he merely spun his index finger. The crowd caught on to the joke and cheered—he literally had them wrapped around his little finger.

A Baptist preacher in Jacksonville called for special services in which he had the teenagers in his congregation pray for Elvis's soul. A picture of the preacher, a Bible in one hand, a poster of Elvis in the other, appeared that next week in *Life* magazine. This upset Gladys especially. She could not reconcile herself to the many ways in which their family's life had changed. The success she had dreamed of turned out to be only half a fantasy, but half fishbowl nightmare as well. Although her alcoholism had grown acute, she saw many things the rest of the family missed. She distrusted the Colonel, particularly. Vernon was blinded by the greenbacks.

Elvis tried to make his mother's fears disappear. He started talking of buying a "farm." He had already moved his family twice: first into a rental property on the appropriately named Getwell Street, and then into a suburban home he purchased on Audubon Drive. With the house under siege from his fans twenty-four hours a day, they needed more privacy. They soon found Graceland, an antebellum fieldstone mansion with a Greek portico, located in Whitehaven, a then largely undeveloped suburb of Memphis. They would take up residence in May.

On October 24, *Variety* carried an article that estimated Elvis's earnings for the year at more than a million dollars, a monumental sum for the time. In terms of popularity and finances, Elvis had arrived.

Even some critics were beginning to warm up to him. The music critic of the *New York Times,* John C. Wilson, said: "The overwhelming nature of the arrival of Elvis Presley as a national figure has tended to overshadow what should be the heart of the matter—his music." He went on to praise Elvis's talent, calling it "incisive if somewhat distinct."

Elvis's fellow musicians were less reserved. Burl Ives commented, "This boy's got a lot of voltage." And the great Louis Armstrong, hearing that Elvis wanted to cut a record with him, said, "You'd be surprised what we could do together."

On October 27, an article appeared on the first page of *Billboard* magazine that contained news which threatened all this good fortune. The story supposedly originated at Fort Dix, New Jersey, where "informed sources" said that Elvis was to be inducted into the army that December. He would be given special furloughs to complete the film work he had already contracted. He would be joining the Special Services and continue performing, Uncle Sam's conscripted entertainer.

This article caused a furor immediately after it appeared. A lot of people did not like Elvis, and the thought of his receiving special treatment from the army provoked the ire of just about the entire VFW. The army steadfastly denied any such intentions. The Memphis draft board in charge of Elvis's case had only just recently sent him a questionnaire, a preliminary to status designation.

Some have questioned whether the Colonel planted the story. Growing more and more independent, Elvis may have been worrying his manager. He had purchased Graceland without consulting the Colonel, and he was obviously chafing about the Colonel's management of his film career. The Colonel might have seen the army induction story as a way of changing Elvis's image from teenage rebel to All-American entertainer. More mainstream—bigger audience. The Colonel would have been an unlikely one, though, to have precipitated Elvis's being stationed overseas. That's no move for a manager without a passport. The Colonel certainly did use Elvis's stint in the army to reposition Elvis more in the center of the entertainment world.

The *Billboard* article included a mysterious line about Elvis's intention to have some gum work done once he was inducted. Some have taken this for a Mafia code—a way of saying that he had better cooperate if he wanted to keep his teeth. To the Colonel's credit, Elvis was kept far away from any Mafia influences, unlike many entertainers, particularly those associated with Las Vegas.

Perhaps the article was only an example of malicious mischief. It reminded everybody, though, that in the late 1950s the draft was compulsory, something Elvis would have to face eventually. His impending enlistment would be a turning point. Perhaps he would be forgotten when he came back. From the top of that mountain he had climbed, Elvis needed not the wheedling voice of the Colonel in his ear, but the chance Solomon received to ask for wisdom.

# 5

---

# A Dogface's Life

O n March 24, 1958, Elvis was inducted into the army. The *Billboard* story ensured that the Memphis draft board would pursue Elvis's case strictly by the book. Some board members, according to records, took a certain pleasure in taking away Elvis's newfound wealth and standing. The head of the draft board was quoted as saying: "After all, when you take him out of the entertainment business, what have you got left? A truck driver."

Elvis had time to accept special deals offered by the Marines and the Navy, though. He could have enlisted in these branches of the service, and spent his time being treated like a VIP. He also could have joined the Special Services of the army and done his hitch entertaining the troops.

Colonel Parker influenced him to accept the common lot of draftees. The Colonel saw the day when Elvis would reemerge from army life as an All-American young man, his image scoured of any juvenile delinquency taint. How many Americans fervently believed that going into the army would make a man of anyone? The Colonel wanted his boy to receive the full benefit of these feelings. It worked out, in fact, as he had planned, although the question remains whether Elvis was well served by this severing of his rock 'n' roll roots. Rock would soon become the mainstream. The Colonel's homogenized ambitions for Elvis placed him on the sidelines of the '60s rock revolution.

The Colonel arranged for Elvis's indoctrination at Fort Chaffee, Arkansas, to be a media circus, with his physical examination, aptitude tests, haircut, and his new wardrobe of army fatigues filmed and photographed as no other "common man" in the army's history. After three days, Lieutenant Colonel Marjorie Schultern finally kicked the Colonel and the media out of Fort Chaffee.

The army shipped Elvis to Fort Hood in central Texas for basic training. After basic, he had another eight weeks of advance training as a crewman for tank warfare. His training completed, he was shipped off to Germany, where his unit would rotate into the Third Armored Division.

Elvis did undertake all the training and duties of the enlisted man. His wealth, though, allowed for some differences in his living arrangements. Fort Hood was an open base. Elvis could receive visitors when he was off duty. His weekend passes allowed him to decamp to other quarters. So he first rented a trailer and then a small house in nearby Killeen, Texas. He brought his parents and paternal grandmother, Minnie Mae (Dodger), down to live there, and had his girlfriend, Anita Wood, come down every weekend along with buddies like Red West, Earl Greenwood, and Lamar Fike. His fans besieged the house, too, and there were always enough people around for a party. He was able to transport much of his world to his new locations.

Soon after Elvis's mother, Gladys, took up residence in Killeen, her health seriously deteriorated. She was suffering from hepatitis. At first her symptoms hinted at gallstones. Her local doctor did not diagnose the illness as hepatitis even after her skin turned yellow. Once diagnosed, her physicians remained stumped as to its cause. Her entire family kept her drinking a close secret. Today, with the publicity given to alcoholism and its many famous victims, a doctor would have to be incredibly uninformed not to perceive that Gladys was a not-so-hidden drinker. In the late 1950s doctors were reticent to come to such conclusions, perhaps because they had little more idea than the average family member how to address the problem. Gladys confined herself more and more to her bedroom, until in the first week of August, it became clear that she needed hospitalization.

Elvis drove Vernon and Gladys to Fort Worth on August 8, a Friday, where they boarded a train for Memphis. Arriving home, Gladys went immediately to see her doctor. That same day she was admitted to Methodist Hospital. Her condition deteriorated steadily over the weekend, despite the care she was now receiving.

Elvis applied for emergency leave and flew into Memphis on Tuesday, August 12. Elvis went to Gladys's side from the airport and then spent the next day with her. When she first saw him, she screamed, "Oh my son!" in a loud voice. She seemed to rally Wednesday, and ordered him to go home about nine in the evening, to get some rest. The doctors finally told him that his mother was suffering from acute hepatitis and liver damage. Her condition was critical.

Vernon called Graceland in the early hours of Thursday morning. Premonitions awoke Elvis with a shock, and he took the call. "She [Gladys] woke me up struggling," he said. "She was suffering for breath. I got to her as quick as I could and the nurse and doctor put her in an oxygen tent. But it was too late."

Evidently, her body traumatized by toxins, Gladys suffered a heart attack. No autopsy was performed. The family knew well enough the source of their misery and wanted to keep the matter private.

Elvis hated drinking. Most biographers have seen this as the wisdom he gained from watching alcohol ruin the careers of other musicians. He had much more personal reasons, though. He saw Gladys's uncontrolled drinking escalate through the years until it finally killed her. Gladys used alcohol as "medicine" to control her nerves. Elvis would make the mistake of indicting the "medicine" rather than his mother's behavior, for he also would have his "medications" to control his nerves.

If we can extend our sympathies to Elvis as an adult child of an alcoholic, we might consider for a moment that Gladys was a victim of the way her family had taught her to resolve conflict. Her mother had been an invalid, using sickness as a means of control, always manipulating those around her rather than confronting their common problems head on. The sins of the fathers are truly inherited to the third generation and beyond, until someone breaks these patterns and finds better ways to deal with conflict and negative emotions.

Gladys put her faith in changing her outward circumstances. For all her church going—and I'm sure she practiced her religion the best she knew how—she was not able to adequately apply the truth of her faith: The rain falls on the just and the unjust, but the person of righteousness, the person who walks with the Lord, experiences a change of heart, an *interior* change, that allows him or her to be grateful in any circumstance. Apparently, Gladys's capacity for contentment declined proportionately to the increase in her material wealth. She saw that improvements in her material circumstances were not going to make her happy, and when this working principle of her hope proved false, she could only find comfort by numbing her emotions.

Grief must be the most difficult of all human emotions, and Gladys's death plunged Elvis into to its blackest depths. When the body was returned to Graceland, Elvis sat on the front steps, paralyzed by his suffering. He told a newsman, "She's all we lived for. She was always my best girl." He cried uncontrollably throughout the day.

Gladys lay for the viewing in her silver casket in the living room. She wore a new baby blue dress. Elvis covered her body with his own, hugging and kissing her, half-rocking her in his arms, mumbling in the baby-talk they had always shared. He called her Satnin', and he pointed out how beautiful her "itty-bitty sooties," her feet, looked to his girlfriend, Anita Wood.

After a funeral in Memphis the next day, arranged by the publicity-minded Colonel, the cortege went out to the burial site. After the service there, Elvis fell on the casket, crying, "Oh, Satnin', I wanna go with you! I don't want to stay here! I can't be without you!" A long time passed before his friends convinced him to come away.

Grief causes overwhelming emotions in anybody, and most of us are far too reserved in expressing it. Elvis's wailing and crying might be looked at as "unmanly" by many. Most of the world, however, has responded to death in exactly this fashion throughout history. Wailing is appropriate. No, the thing that strikes me as unique about Elvis's grief comes from his telltale statements. Was his mother really all he lived for?

The simple answer is no, obviously. He wanted his own happiness in spite of how much he loved her and still needed her in his life. Elvis seemed to suffer as much from guilt as he did from loss when Gladys died. When he became successful and attended to the requirements of his burgeoning career, many of which took him away from his mother, he must have felt guilty about succeeding at the very thing they had dreamed of. The reality of the situation, unlike their dreams, only allowed for Elvis himself to be in the spotlight. They were two, not one. What's more, he wanted his own way—to be his own person even as hard as it was to grow up and break away.

He must have suffered severely from false guilt—the feeling that he had somehow been responsible for his mother's death. Of course, he wasn't. He had the normal thoughts that many people in similar situations have had; if he had been there, maybe he could have helped. Unfortunately, Elvis could not see this. His mind transformed this unacceptable guilt into anger against God, a typical human reaction when facing inexplicable tragedy.

Someone had to be at fault. He suspected he was, but he was willing to blame God. He couldn't consider that Gladys was responsible for her own death—the hard truth.

Elvis loved his mother. No one can deny that. But her death should have given him an opportunity to rethink the bargains he had made in life. To find happiness in some other way than pleasing others and changing his outward circumstances, to find an identity of his own apart from Gladys. No one around him, though, was capable even of suggesting these things. His family watched him suffer, comforted him, but like Elvis himself, they were never able to address the problem.

As might be expected, the problem quickly found a way to reconstitute itself. Elvis was tragically dependent on his mother's love. When he was denied her love, he went in search of something to replace it. To the very end of his life, he kept up his search, but tragically, he was looking for love in all the wrong places.

His life in the army quickly demanded, however, that he put one foot in front of another and get on with his life. His battalion arrived in Germany on the SS *General Randall* on October 1, 1958. They went directly from the ship to Ray Barracks in Friedberg, an hour's drive northeast of Frankfurt.

Elvis's family, Vernon and Dodger, and his friends, Lamar Fike and Red West, followed after him, establishing a household in Bad Nauheim, an old spa town. Its narrow cobblestone streets wind past Victorian buildings with high-pitched roofs, quaint towers, spires, and lacy weather vanes. Elvis acquired a large BMW, which became known in the press as the *Elviswagen*.

Elvis did well in the army and served with distinction. He resorted to his Humes High personality, one of the fellows, a willing and eager team player. Privately, he might have been in agony about the years the army was taking away from him. In his duties, he stuck to business and perhaps even enjoyed being valued for what he could contribute rather than the person, or image, he had become in the public's eye. He worked as part of a tank crew and then drove a jeep, as well as doing guard duty.

He met several men during this time who would become a part of his traveling crew, including Joe Esposito, the crew chief I worked under years later.

Currie Grant, another new friend, a noncommissioned officer in the Special Services, brought a fourteen-year-old girl by the house in Bad Neuheim one night. Elvis staged get-togethers on the weekend for his old friends and new army buddies. His intimates brought girls they thought Elvis might like. This evening, Elvis looked up and saw an angel of a girl, Priscilla Beaulieu.

He guessed she must be a junior or senior in high school.

She told him she was in the ninth grade.

He exclaimed about that and started laughing. "Why, you're just a baby," he said.

"Thanks," she said, offended.

"Well, seems the little girl has spunk," he said, recovering. He flashed her that grinning, yet warm smile of his.

Then he went to the piano and started singing for his guests. He sang "Rags to Riches" and "Are You Lonesome Tonight?" His friends joined him on the harmonies in "End of the Rainbow." He did a Jerry Lee Lewis impression, hammering at the keys so hard that a glass of water started walking off the top of the piano. The singer caught it in mid-air without missing a beat, to his guests' delight.

Priscilla felt shy. She noticed a Brigitte Bardot poster on the wall. She could hardly look at Elvis. But then she noticed that her reluctance to meet his eye drew his attentions to her more and more. Soon he was performing just for her.

Later he spoke with her alone in the kitchen. When Currie came by to take Priscilla home, Elvis protested—he wanted her to stay just a little longer. Before she left that night he mentioned that she would have to come again soon.

Elvis began seeing Priscilla regularly from then on. She was the stepdaughter of a captain in the air force, Paul Beaulieu, who was stationed nearby at Wiesbaden. The captain required Elvis to come by not too long after the couple started dating, ostensibly to ask him about the escort-delivery system he had instituted (Vernon or Lamar most often drove Priscilla back and forth to his house in Bad Neuheim), but really to sound out his intentions.

Elvis brought Vernon along for moral support when he met the Beaulieus. Elvis wore his uniform, yessired Captain Beaulieu, and, without making any promises, indicated that ultimately he looked forward to a conventional life with a wife and children. He charmed Priscilla's parents. They let her pursue this "chance of a lifetime."

Elvis felt he could talk to Priscilla as he could few others. He confessed to her how much he missed his mother. Priscilla calls Gladys the love of Elvis's life in her book, a surprising admission from the only woman who became his wife. He told her his mother would have liked her as much as he did—a way of confessing to the identity he found between them, or establishing one, or giving himself permission to extend his love for Gladys through Priscilla. He confessed to the guilt he felt over her death; he had not been with her enough when she became ill. He thought she could not understand that peace had come to Europe and that he would not be in danger in the service. She saw his conscription as the "war thing." He told Priscilla how he called his mother every day from the road. She could not sleep until he did. Once, when his car caught fire in the middle of the night, Gladys sat straight up in bed, waking out of a dead sleep, and screamed. Their connection was that strong.

Elvis also told Priscilla about his mother's drinking, but instead of seeing this as the cause of her death, he attributed it to her depression at his impending departure—to her fear of losing him, the fatal error the whole family made concerning her drinking.

Elvis and Priscilla spent hours in his room alone, but Elvis did not make love to Priscilla, according to her, until their marriage. He believed, he told her, in the sanctity of marriage and the sacred character of sex within marriage.

This has been hard for many people to believe. Elvis's promiscuity has been well documented, but I believe Priscilla.

Elvis inherited the double standard that it's all right to exploit women who are willing to be exploited. Those who demand respect, receive it. It's not a great standard. It's certainly not a Christian standard.

On the other hand, Elvis's hypocrisy may be preferable to the cynicism advocated by many. At least Elvis did not lose sight entirely of the monogamous ideal. He refused to see, though, how his promiscuity impaired his will to live up to his ideals—ideals that had been *taught* to him by his Christian upbringing and *caught* by him from his relationship with his mother. Even after her death, Gladys would be with him.

One of the ways Gladys was with him for the rest of his life affected all his relationships with the opposite sex; she would remain the most important woman in his life. This prevented him from establishing a primary relationship with another woman.

Since he never quite grew up, he conducted his relationships as a matter of extending the original pattern rather than reestablishing a new pattern. This is what I mean: People who have truly grown up, emotionally as well as physically, appreciate how the differences between people make for healthy relationships, first between our parents and ourselves, and then others and ourselves. Opposites attract because healthy people recognize the need to be completed in their mates, to include within a larger whole those aspects of character that are opposite to their own. They understand unity-in-difference. They like the other person for *not* being just like them. People like Elvis, in their deepest motivations, tend to turn their mates into reflections of themselves; they want to see themselves in another in order to feel that their life is valid. And Elvis tried to turn Priscilla, at least for a time, into a virtual mirror image of himself.

Almost any man can be momentarily attracted to a fourteen-year-old, at least one with Priscilla's beauty. But it takes a particular kind of man to mold someone to his own specifications, to pursue a fourteen-year-old the way Elvis did. Elvis later confessed to another girlfriend, Linda Thompson, "I tried to mold her into what I wanted. I realized too late that you just can't do that."

He never realized that you cannot find a mirror image either, and you should not try. To the end, with his last girlfriend, Ginger Alden, he looked for another girl who reminded him of Gladys, or at least one whom his mother would approve. In romance, he grew up a lot, particularly through his divorce from Priscilla and his relationship with Linda Thompson, but he never quite got it; he kept making the same mistakes. But isn't that something most people could say about their romantic lives?

Vernon seemed to recover from his own grief over his wife's death relatively quickly. After all, he had been living with a woman whose alcoholism made him more a caretaker than a full-fledged spouse. During the winter of 1958–59, Vernon met my parents, Sergeant Bill Stanley, a decorated veteran who had been George Patton's personal bodyguard, and my mother, Dee.

My folks were having marital difficulties at the time. My father was one of those hard-drinking, hard-living lifers. He would have reached a much higher position in the service if he had not been an alcoholic. He had plenty of courage, but not enough self-control.

My mother asked Elvis to dinner, out of curiosity, I suppose, and as a gesture of friendship. Elvis countered with an offer to have coffee at his hotel and sent his father as a substitute. My mother must have poured out her problems to Vernon. Even my dad, for a time, looked to Vernon as a mediator of the family's disputes.

But, as often happens, the family friend becomes a spouse's romantic interest. My mother, Dee, and Vernon took up together. My two brothers, David and Billy, and I were living with our parents at the time in Wiesbaden. (I was only five years old, so I don't remember much of this.)

As I understand it, my father was so beset with the problems his drinking had gotten him into, that his capacity to fight for his marriage and family was limited. Although it caused him great pain, he let go of his wife and three boys, thinking that Dee and Vernon might well be able to do a better job of raising us than he could.

My mother took us home to the States and put us in a "residential" boarding school, Breezy Point Farms, in Virginia. In some ways it was no better than a typical orphanage, but most of the kids did have parents. There we waited in the wings to enter the story I've been telling.

I inherited in the next few years, in one form or another, all the love, pain, and ways of fitting into the world that I've recounted here. It's taken me Elvis's lifetime and the fifteen years since his death, though, to manage as much perspective as I have on it now. As I child, I was about to be strapped into the Elvis roller coaster, and the momentum of our rush down that first big hill took us on the fastest possible ride with what seemed at the time an unlimited supply of tickets.

# 6

# My Brother, My Father, My Hero

*I* came into Elvis's life when he was twenty-five, a movie star, and the conquering hero of millions of young women who had eagerly awaited his return from the army. Now that he was back, having served his country honorably, even the parents of America looked upon him with pride. Elvis was at the height of his power. He moved in a world very few adults have ever seen, a world more like those of fabled princes and potentates than that of twentieth-century people. He had made his comic book superhero dreams a reality.

I was a fitting subject for this superhero's rescue, a little boy stashed away with his two brothers in what proved to be an impersonal boarding school. Although Breezy Point Farms occupied an impressive estate on the banks of a river, and while the administrators were nice to us when our mother was present, we were treated quite differently when she left. We were referred to as army brats by the other kids, who were mostly older than we.

We had to sleep in a cold, dark dormitory. Even though David was only three, he had to sleep across the hall from Billy and me. This was especially traumatic for him because we had slept together all our lives. Here we were separated not only from our parents but from each other as well.

At night when the lights went out I could hear him crying, so Billy and I took turns sneaking across the hall to sit on his cot until he fell asleep. Sometimes we would have to crawl into bed with him to comfort him. Whenever we were caught, we were punished by the sour, sickly looking teachers. They poured Tabasco sauce into our mouths for this and other routine infractions.

We ended up calling Breezy Point "the orphanage" among ourselves, which expressed how abandoned we felt. If anybody, I needed, like Freddy Freeman, a Captain Marvel to rescue me from the bad guys.

Christmas came and all the other kids left for the holidays. No one even came to visit us, and we felt terribly alone and abandoned. Mom called on Christmas Day to tell us she was in Germany with Vernon and she wished we were there.

By the time Mom called in January on Billy's seventh birthday, we were fairly sure we'd never leave. Mom told us about Elvis, and we must have mentioned him to the other kids (even though I didn't know who he was), but they only teased us, thinking that we were making it up.

Finally, one morning all three of us were called to the office before we had finished our chores. What a surprise to see Mom standing there and to find out that Vernon and she had come to take us home.

On the drive to Memphis, Mom explained that Vernon and she were married and that he was our new daddy. She also spent much of the long trip talking about Elvis and his wonderful career. All of this was too much for the three of us to absorb. We weren't allowed to listen to the radio at Breezy Point Farms, so we had never even heard Elvis sing. We were too excited about leaving the hot sauce, the rules, and the mistreatment to think about anything else.

On the drive Vernon impressed me as someone who did not say much, but whose good will I thought genuine. He was doing everything he could to cooperate with my mother's plans and provide for our needs.

Imagine what it was like to see Graceland for the first time. My first impression lingers even after all these years. It sits atop a hill overlooking fourteen rolling acres of fields, profuse with oak and magnolia trees. At the top of the long drive that leads to the front of the mansion there is a low stone wall. The first time we entered the wrought-iron front gates, the famous Music Gates, the house was still a natural-colored limestone built in the colonial style. Elvis later had it painted white and installed soft blue spotlights. We were awed. Vernon explained that this was to be our home.

I was overwhelmed by all the cars in the driveway and my first glimpse of the formal dining room. A white baby grand piano dominated the living room, with its rich, red carpet, purple walls, and gold trim. A winding gold-and-white staircase led to the bedrooms, the music room, and the poolroom.

Then we met Elvis. He welcomed us, gathering us up into his arms. "I always wanted a little brother," he said. "And now I have three!" I was overwhelmed. I grasped immediately how Elvis stood at the center of Graceland's life. He was its sun; everything radiated out from his presence; everyone's path looped outward and back in response to his gravity.

I know now that Elvis resented Vernon's marrying so soon after Gladys's death. The way he felt about his mother, Elvis was probably reluctant to accept a new woman in Vernon's life at anytime. He had the grace, though, not to visit his anger on three defenseless little boys—something a lesser person might well have done. We might have represented the redeeming part of the new arrangement to Elvis, since his first cry of greeting carried his true sentiments: He *had* wanted a younger brother—he pestered his parents about this until they explained Jesse and his birth had resulted in complications for his mother that did not allow her to have more children. Gladys, in fact, miscarried at least once after Elvis's birth. Also, Elvis turned to Vernon in a new way after his mother's death. His father, although he had not been privy to the birth of the dream, actually enjoyed Elvis's success much more than his mother, since he liked its material and social benefits, while Gladys cared more about her influence over Elvis, something his success abated. With Elvis's feeling for *clan,* he took us into his life seemingly without reservation.

For the first few nights we all slept on the floor of Vernon and Mom's bedroom, which was just down the hall from Elvis's room. After that we moved into the garage that had been converted for our use. We lived there for two years.

When we awakened our first morning at Graceland, we were greeted with a veritable wonderland of toys. There were bicycles, tricycles, scooters, sleds, television sets, everything imaginable for the three of us. Elvis had gone shopping and personally selected everything for us. He even had a swing set installed in the yard as we slept.

We had the entire fourteen acres of the estate and the whole wonderful house itself as our play area. There were even peacocks, guinea hens, and mules on the property, as well as the chickens Vernon kept for fresh eggs. The only exception was Elvis's room—that was strictly off-limits.

I can only now imagine the disruptions three young boys must have brought to Graceland. We explored everywhere. We experimented with the phone system, answering it as well as listening in on conversations. Not once did Elvis reprimand us for interrupting him or his sleeping schedule, a schedule much different than we were accustomed to.

Every day we were driven to Graceland School. Sometimes Alberta, the maid, drove us in the pink Cadillac that had belonged to Gladys. Usually Vernon took us, but occasionally Lamar Fike drove us in the BMW, the *Elviswagen*, which Elvis had brought back from Germany. We appreciated his driving more than the others because he drove so fast. We were always anxious to get home to see if Elvis was there.

We loved to sneak up on him and try to knock him down. It was amazing how indulgent he was with us. Vernon was a strong disciplinarian, but there were many times when Elvis talked him out of spanking us or took the blame for us. He wanted us, it seemed, to enjoy the same pampering his mother had extended to him.

There were so many new people in our lives. The house was filled with people. One of the first I met was Aunt Cleatis, Vernon's scary-looking sister-in-law. She looked like a vampire to me, sitting in her chair all alone in the dining room, with her jet-black hair and a tipsy slur in her speech.

We also liked Vester, Vernon's brother. Vester worked the grounds at Graceland and often manned the gate, ushering guests through the crowd of fans that always waited there. Uncle Earl Pritchard, another favorite of ours who was married to Vernon's sister, Nash, worked on the grounds, as well as Travis Smith and his two sons, Billy and Gene.

My particular favorite was Vernon's mother, Minnie Mae. Grandma, or Dodger, as Elvis called her, was tall and thin with dark hair she wore in a bun. I spent many happy hours in Grandma's room, drinking Pepsi and watching soap operas— "her stories"—on television. Elvis would come to visit her quite often and listen to all the advice she gave him about dating and eating right. She kept the money he gave her in a cigar box in her closet and would dole it out to others in need, including me.

My special little job for her was to pick just the right kind of twig from one of the big trees on the property. I would bring several back to her room, and she would show me how to shave off the bark with her little pocket knife. She then used the twig to dip into her snuff can. She would sit with that little twig protruding from her mouth and savor the tobacco. I couldn't wait until I was old enough to dip snuff like Grandma! That this might be a habit formed in the days of the family's poverty as a way of warding off hunger never occurred to me.

As I think back on my first few months at Graceland, I realize what an important source of stability Grandma was for me. She had a schedule I could set my watch by. She always had time for me, always seemed to want me around. Elvis seemed to draw an inner strength and stability from her, too, as would Priscilla later on.

All of our new family made life that much more fun for the three of us. Vernon seemed to be the one who worked at keeping us in line and disciplining us. His responsibility for managing the mansion and its finances made him less tolerant of our shenanigans, but he had a fun-loving nature, too, and he and Elvis never tired of playing jokes on each other and everyone else. I grew to love Vernon and appreciate him, as Elvis did in the years after his mother's death. When their rivalry for Gladys's affections ended, their bond as father and son strengthened as few would have anticipated.

In addition to the various family members there were the members of the "Memphis Mafia," Elvis's special group of friends and assistants. Sonny West was one of our favorites because he played with us and taught us all sorts of useful things. He gave us our first boxing lessons. Jerry Schilling played football with us. Joe Esposito was always kidding around, and Lamar Fike always made us laugh because he looked and acted like Jackie Gleason.

During the time we lived at Graceland, my brothers and I attended Graceland School and later Harding Academy, a private church school. Being a part of the Presley family meant that the other students were curious about us, and we were, inevitably, set apart by our connection with Elvis.

We occasionally fought with other kids when they taunted us, but I also profited during those years by selling Elvis's autograph to the other students. There were the inevitable questions about life with Elvis Presley from my schoolmates, and while this was flattering to me, the ridicule and disparaging remarks from the teachers about our lifestyle was difficult for me to understand.

I remember how smug I felt one day when one of my teachers took me out in the hall and, warning me ahead of time not to mention our conversation to anyone, asked me in a breathless voice what it was like to live with Elvis Presley. Everyone wanted to know, whether they considered it proper or not.

Explaining what life was like with Elvis, especially for a six-year-old boy, was quite a task. Besides Graceland itself, its toys, its multitude of pets—including a monkey, a myna bird, and several dogs—we also had the benefits of the "toys for big boys" that only large amounts of money could buy.

Elvis and his friends loved to revert to the little kids in themselves, and his wealth enabled him to provide wonderful adventures for all of us. He could rent a skating rink, an amusement park like the Fair Grounds (later renamed Libertyland), or a theater, usually the Memphian, for the entire night. The long line of limousines with Elvis in the lead would take off from Graceland for a night that most kids could only dream about. We not only had the entire place to ourselves, but everything was free.

I would make myself ill by eating as many hot dogs, Butterfingers, and ice cream bars as I could stuff down. At Libertyland we could ride the roller coaster as many times as we wanted. We would face off on the bumper cars and help initiate new people into the group by banding together to knock them silly—a bumper car ritual that shocked the initiates with its intensity. Those nights were like kid heaven.

Elvis and his friends would do the craziest stunts, like stepping out of the roller coaster at the top of the hills and waiting for the cars to come around again. Mom must have realized how wild these guys were because there were times when she tried to keep us home, but Elvis would charm her into letting us go. We were always begging him to take our side, and he usually did. We had a real sense of being safe with him no matter how wild the hijinks. As time progressed, Mom became more and more concerned with what we were exposed to.

Soon Mom began to protest against how late Elvis kept us out and started to assert her authority. She was very concerned about our development soon after we arrived at Graceland. Our traumatic early childhood with an alcoholic father, our parents' frequent fights, and our extended stay at Breezy Point Farms made her feel guilty, I'm sure. She seemed to be trying to make up for some of the earlier mistakes she, Bill Stanley, and Vernon had made. She became a zealot of stability and security.

Elvis, it soon became clear, wanted us to have everything he had been denied as a child. He was, in a way, making up for his own lost childhood, and he took particular pleasure in seeing us enjoy the benefits of his success.

Even when it meant going against Elvis's wishes, Vernon would side with Mom when it came to what was best for us boys. Vernon supported Mom in her efforts to establish weekly church attendance. He drove us to the Whitehaven Church of Christ every Sunday morning.

During the drive, Vernon (by now we were calling him Daddy) gave Mom money for the offering, and then slowly pulled up to the church's awning. My mother marched us off to Sunday school and then made her way to her own class with her best friend, Wilma Sparkman. After Sunday school my mother, my brothers, and I would meet at the second (yes, second) row of the church auditorium for the worship service.

The only exciting part of church services for me as a child was communion. Because I had not been baptized, I was not allowed to participate directly. I remember being awestruck as I watched the others consume the elements of bread and wine (grape juice in that denomination), and I wondered what magical or mystical power these people were drawing from the ritual.

When church was over, Daddy picked us up and took us to lunch. Occasionally, Mom put Dad on the spot by asking him to say the blessing. Interestingly enough, when Vernon prayed his words seemed sincere. His religious beliefs still meant something to him, it was clear, even though in terms of church practice he had drawn away from the habits that had once made him the head deacon of his church in Tupelo.

Elvis's lifestyle and his influence on us was decidedly more secular and worldly than my mother wanted. She became more and more convinced that we were being lured away from the path she had chosen for us.

There were several incidents that only confirmed her worst fears. One that especially alarmed her happened when I was playing at the mansion with Gene Smith's daughter, Biddie. We were only six or seven at the time and were exploring the bedroom areas upstairs. This was before the entire upstairs area was enclosed to make a private retreat for Elvis.

We ventured into one of the rooms and began jumping on the bed, trying to touch the ceiling. After tiring of this, I began thumbing through the magazines on the nightstand by the bed. I had never seen a *Playboy* before, and the pictures provoked my curiosity. Biddie felt the same way when I showed her the photographs. We thought the pictures were funny and began laughing delightedly at each other.

Mother, Alberta, and Biddie's mom must have heard the commotion and ran to see what could be so entertaining to us.

Finding us in a crumpled bed with a *Playboy* magazine was not nearly as amusing to them as it had been for us. My mother practically went into hysterics. Her concern over how corrupt I was becoming only escalated.

Even though Elvis told the guys that they were going to have to be more discreet with their magazines and such, the party atmosphere at Graceland and particularly the unmarried guys and their girlfriends who spent the night with them were sending a definite message to me and to my brothers about relationships and lifestyles. We had Mom carting us off to church at every chance, and then we had all the excitement and glamour of life at the mansion.

In the midst of this running contest for control between Elvis and my Mom, my parents decided it would be best if we had our own home. So my two brothers and I moved with my parents to a three-bedroom house in the subdivision that was being developed close to Graceland. Our modest, yet pretty, white provincial house was very nice. It sat nestled amid big oak and birch trees.

Still, I was devastated by the move. I loved exploring Graceland and hanging out with Elvis and the guys. So did my brothers. But the move was particularly heartwrenching to me. My brothers will tell you—they have written this, in fact, in their books—that Mom, and Vernon after her, disciplined me more strictly than they did Billy and David. My mother was harder on me, as if she resented me, which I think she did. My brothers, trying to be charitable, have suggested that Mom felt I was the most gifted, both intellectually and socially, and so she expected more of me. She drove me so that I would produce.

I would like to think this so, but I am persuaded now that something more common and less generous influenced my mother. I came along within a year after my elder brother's birth. My parents were probably deep into their own troubles at this time, and I'm sure that my mother resented being pregnant. She might get out of the marriage with one child, she must have been thinking, but how could she escape with two? Caring for her newborn, she experienced morning sickness, her legs' swelling, and the other discomforts of pregnancy with me. My birth gave her as little joy as carrying me, and she fell into a pattern of taking out her unconscious anger on me in little ways that accumulated over time into virtual oppression. People are people. This happens. This was not right, but now, as an adult, I can understand it. Then, I simply longed for the surrogate family structure I enjoyed with Elvis and Grandma—my father recast as a young hero, and my mother transformed into a figure of pure benevolence and unconditional love. You can see why I loved being at Graceland.

To ease my pain, and the similar feelings of my brothers, Vernon would periodically take us back to Graceland to visit Grandma, see the guys, or enjoy special occasions.

Elvis made ordinary days seem special to me. I loved to watch him eat the huge breakfasts that Alberta, the cook, prepared for him. I was content just to sit with him while he watched his favorite game shows like "Password," and the shows hosted by his friend and fellow Memphian, Wink Martindale. He loved to sit and lean against the stereo while listening to the recordings of John Gary, Jackie Wilson, and various gospel groups.

When we first arrived at Graceland, Elvis was dating Anita Wood, and the two of them spent hours in the afternoon on his Harley 74 chopper. His spectacular way of starting his motorcycle with a karate kick was fascinating to me.

In fact, he was very accomplished at martial arts, and watching him break boards inspired me to try it myself. After almost breaking my hand several times, I decided to stick to balsa wood and popsicle sticks.

Our first Christmas at Graceland is a vivid memory for me.

Elvis's childlike enthusiasm was contagious. It was his favorite time of year. The groundskeepers stationed a nativity scene and lights on the front lawn. They brought in a huge tree and placed it in the dining room on the right side of the house. The tree was usually seven to eight feet tall.

I still remember that first Christmas in 1960 as I participated in the decorating, hanging brilliant metallic red, blue, and gold balls on the tree and adding the tinsel. We, of course, made a contest of throwing on the tinsel, and Elvis let me win. The tree trimming was an all-out effort that lasted long into the night.

After strings of lights had been added, we made quite a ceremony of lighting the tree. Elvis asked several times if we were all ready. He waited, asked us again, waited some more, and then finally satisfied our curiosity, our "ahs" filling the room with the vast array of colored light.

Each day during the holiday season gifts poured in from fans all over the world, and the mounds of presents grew and grew. I couldn't believe all the presents. On Christmas Eve the gifts would be opened. Elvis personally opened each one, and if there happened to be a story attached to the present, Vernon would tell us who sent the present and why. Elvis had touched the lives of many people through his songs, and he was really humbled by the outpouring of love he received in the form of their gifts to him.

After Elvis had opened the many gifts he received from his fans and record and movie producers, he would turn to the gifts that those close to him had bought. Then my brothers and I opened the wonderful gifts we received. Last of all, Vernon, Mom, and (that first Christmas) Anita opened theirs.

New Year's Eve involved a completely different sort of celebration. Grown men armed themselves with fireworks, football or motorcycle helmets, gloves, and goggles and waged war throughout the night. They'd use roman candles and shot bursts of flame the size of a golf ball in the direction of their opponents. Throughout the grounds, the small comets flashed over the lawns, and the sounds of buzz bombs and chasers reverberated off Graceland's walls.

One year someone accidentally set the house on fire. Elvis called everyone together and said to cool it because the fire department had been called and was on their way. While he spoke, he slipped a buzz bomb into the large box of fireworks without any of us noticing. He walked away with a smug smile on his face and then laughed uproariously as the ensuing explosion caused everyone to scatter. Poor Dad was left with the unpleasant task of explaining to the fire marshall that he would get things under control.

As everyone knows, Elvis dated many beautiful women. Anita Wood was the first one I came to know. I liked her. For one thing, she was beautiful, five foot four, big brown eyes, blonde hair (at the time), and shapely legs. Everyone approved of her, especially Grandma.

Anita was a star in her own right. She had her own radio and television program in Memphis during the mid and late '50s. She would play the top ten rock 'n' roll or rhythm and blues songs, conduct telephone interviews, and show the latest dance craze. Occasionally she would sing in her pretty alto voice.

But she was not stuck up. She made everyone feel important, and although she had the run of Graceland, she treated the employees with respect and courtesy.

She loved Elvis—even as a child I could see that. She was dating Elvis when Gladys passed away, and she provided an important source of strength for him at that time.

Anita was not dependent upon Elvis like so many others that he dated. She had a career, paid her own bills, and was capable of doing what she pleased. This made her something like his equal, and their relationship was healthier than any he would know with his other girlfriends.

Anita was one of the few who could deal with Elvis's fame while enjoying the attention and admiration he received. She did not appear threatened or resentful when she saw Elvis linked with his costars on the cover of movie magazines. Perhaps her independence and self-assurance sustained her through what could have been a very difficult time in their relationship. She even turned a blind eye to beauties like Juliet Prowse, the South African dancer who starred with Elvis in *G.I. Blues*. She could share Elvis with these women on the screen. But one thing she would not do is share her place with him at Graceland.

In looking back at these events, I've had to wonder why Elvis ever turned to Priscilla. I know now that he complained of

Anita's independence to Priscilla when they started dating in Germany. It should be pointed out that Elvis was not *that much* of a mama's boy; he had a number of relationships with independent-minded women like Anita. When it came down to it, though, it does seem that he craved making the women he loved over in his own image.

I remember when Anita was being displaced by Priscilla. I remember the fight Elvis and she had about it. He actually tried to maintain his relationship with Anita even as he became more serious about Priscilla. In 1961, he brought Priscilla over from Germany to visit him at Christmas. He wanted Anita to share the holiday with Priscilla, letting Elvis be with Priscilla for some days, and Anita coming back when Priscilla went home.

Anita would have none of that, of course.

They began their discussion as they sat together at the kitchen counter. Before long they were yelling at the top of their lungs, and their discussion had disintegrated into throwing plates, glasses, and cups onto the floor. I was standing outside the swinging door to the kitchen listening to them, when Daddy walked in expecting to eat lunch. He grabbed me around the waist and whisked me out through the back door.

I later came back into the house to find Elvis and Anita hugging and saw him gently kiss her on the forehead. I never saw them together again.

I liked Priscilla from the moment I met her when she came to spend the holidays that Christmas of 1961, and she seemed to like me back. I thought she was the prettiest girl I'd ever met. She was ten years younger than Elvis and seemed very shy. She was very polite to my mom and dad, and soon became comfortable around my brothers and me.

She went back to Germany after the holidays, and in late January Elvis left to film *Fun in Acapulco*. After the film was completed, he returned to Graceland, bringing Priscilla with him.

Priscilla's stepfather, Captain Beaulieu, arrived a short time later and spent several days grilling Elvis and my father about the arrangements for Priscilla. It was decided that she would move into the house with us on Hermitage Street. She was to attend Immaculate Conception High, a private school, where she would be required to wear a uniform. The rules for Priscilla were to be just like the ones Vernon set for us boys; she faced stringent requirements about visitors, spending money, use of the car, etc. These rules largely disappeared after Captain Beaulieu left. Priscilla moved into the mansion after only a few weeks, the promises to Captain Beaulieu notwithstanding.

Priscilla was competitive and very much a tomboy. She loved to race us or compete in any kind of athletic contest. She even cheated like a boy, pushing me down or tackling me at the start of a race to gain an advantage. We spent a lot of time together while Elvis was away making movies. I came to have quite a crush on her.

She wanted to go on location with Elvis, of course, but she was in school, and Elvis was careful to keep her away from some of the stars and starlets he was linked with in the press.

In her efforts to compete with the beautiful actresses Elvis met, 'Cilla, as Elvis and then the rest of the family called her, worked at changing her appearance. She began dying her hair and using lots of mascara, yet underneath she was still a teenager. She had lots of time on her hands with Elvis gone so much and very few friends with whom to spend that time. She was living what I know now must have been an uncomfortably isolated life.

The friends she did have were carefully scrutinized by Elvis and Daddy.

When she couldn't find a friend to go to the movies with her, I would get a call. I was always ready to go anywhere with her. She had a fondness for horror movies, and many times we would watch a movie several times in one night.

Six years after she arrived at Graceland, on May 1, 1967, Priscilla and Elvis were married in Las Vegas at the Aladdin Hotel. The wedding and all the arrangements were made by Colonel Parker. Vernon and Mom attended, but I didn't know anything about it until afterward.

Elvis and Priscilla did throw a big reception at Graceland later in the month, and all the people excluded by the Colonel were invited. I sat at the reception table by Priscilla, talking with her animatedly. She was so beautiful; she captivated every bit of my attention. Suddenly, I heard the rest of the table laughing. Someone had made a remark about my being jealous—my crush on Priscilla was an open secret—and then everyone turned to see that Priscilla and I had not heard the remark, which confirmed it, and cracked everybody up.

Marriage changed Priscilla. It gave her license to take control as the mistress of Graceland. Marriage also entitled her to keep a closer watch over the rumors that filtered into the press about Elvis and his costars. She became skeptical and a bit controlling. She had the right, but a gradual change would have been easier to take.

Her new attitude bothered me at the time. Being kept at arm's length and considered a rival for Elvis's affections—as she considered almost everyone in those days—was painful. I'm sure she felt overwhelmed by all the people jockeying for position around Elvis and apprehension over everybody's demands on him.

Now I can see that she had a right to assume new prerogatives. She might well have been less insistent about asserting her authority if Elvis had given her the respect any man owes his wife. But he wanted her to continue fitting in as one of the gang—an unreasonable expectation, I'd say now. He also thought she should be content to be the mistress of Graceland, his loving wife, and not ask too many questions about his other liaisons—an outrageous expectation.

I had my own false expectations. After Priscilla saw that her capacity to change Elvis would be limited and she relaxed her hold over access to him, I spent an increasing amount of time with the two of them. Often, during the warm months, they would invite me, just me, over for a pool party. Sometimes we talked over family matters, and I remember confessing to them how worried I was about the tensions developing between

Vernon and Mom. If they divorced, I'd be exiled, I thought, from Elvis and Priscilla's life.

They assured me that would never happen. They actually said they would take care of me if my parents divorced, and I could come and live with them. I cannot be sure how much they meant this, at least in any literal sense. I did feel confident at the time that Elvis and Priscilla were ready to serve as a second family for me. They understood my problems at home. They saw my treatment as unfair—even Priscilla, who had much more heart-felt respect for discipline than Elvis.

My brother Billy made an interesting observation. "We had two daddies," he said. "Vernon would tell us what we couldn't do and Elvis would tell us what we could do." I felt the need for another father and mother even more keenly than my brothers. In my own mind, I regarded Elvis as a father, an older brother, and my own personal hero.

It's not too much to say that I started living my life as an extension of his. I'm not Elvis, I can say with relief and gratitude at last, but much of my psychological formation paralleled his. With a brother I could never live up to, I, too, found my own Captain Marvel fantasy and yearned to become the most powerful boy in the world while thinking my happiness lay not in exercising my own gifts but in *pleasing* someone else.

Many family attitudes other than those of Elvis and Priscilla themselves encouraged this response. We were always cautioned to be on our best behavior because everything we did reflected not on ourselves, we were told, but on Elvis. Vernon especially sought to inspire this attitude. People in the outside world seemed to agree. They treated us differently when they claimed to be treating us the same, because they would never have had to make a point of this "equal treatment" if the treatment had not been unequal from the beginning. Some things are unavoidable—tensions that are there whether anyone likes them or not.

So, as I entered my teenage years, I tried to emulate Elvis in everything I did. If I was going to be like him, I was also going to work that angle to the max. I felt entitled to the privileges he enjoyed—all of them—because I shared his public scrutiny.

Unrealistic? Crazy? Self-destructive? Of course. But the chain had already caught the roller coaster car and we were poised at the top of that first big hill.

# 7

## The Impersonal Life

*I* was thrust into Elvis's life at a time, I can see in retrospect, at which Elvis was already plunging into his head-spinning future. The army had already changed him in ways that had far-ranging consequences in his public and private lives. He may have taken pep pills, or speed, before his army days, as part of his fast-paced life in the early days of his career. But his reliance on amphetamines became an established habit in Germany. This made him more irritable and given to excess and insomnia, and also insidiously suggested the need for more drugs to counter these unwanted effects. This needs to be mentioned first, because most who have written about Elvis note his drug taking and then largely forget this when they evaluate his behavior. Even at this time in his life, in the early 1960s, the effects of the drugs gave an edge to Elvis's temper and begin to diminish his will, and most importantly, *started to rob him of hope.*

He feared returning to Graceland after his mother's death. When he bought the home, he thought of it as the realization of the dream they had shared of owning a farm. Graceland would always be haunted with Gladys's memory, as Elvis's life would be. He had lived so much for her that he must have wondered how to go on. He had already achieved the success they envisioned, and more. He understood, too, that this had not made Gladys happy. In his own mind his success had taken him away from his mother, and these separations seemed to have contributed to her death. He grieved for her sincerely, that's without question. But I wonder, too, if part of his grief contained anger. People are often angry at their loved ones for "leaving" them, or at God for taking these people from them. Elvis's spirit must have been devastated at the realization that he had been motivated in many ways by his love for his mother, and now she was gone. What would motivate him now? What to do? What did he want?

Elvis came relatively late to that question in life. He had a gift, and he set out to use it, but he remained bewildered by its larger purpose and demands. He wanted to be his family's hero and take them out of poverty. He succeeded. But then much more difficult questions cropped up. What happens when you get what you want in life? What does getting what you want mean? And even if you know the answers to these questions, how do you find the strength to keep on exercising your gifts when necessity no longer sends its adrenaline rush coursing through your veins?

Most of us, when faced with a crisis, instead of truly changing, seek to reestablish what we're familiar with, including, ironically, our old problems. The key to real change, however, is to confront the things we are most afraid of. Those things often look like external circumstances, but they are really interior dispositions—how we think and feel about ourselves, and what we do in response to those feelings.

Elvis was afraid of not being loved. It was about that simple, although this may seem simple-minded to some, too simplistic to others. It may also seem impossible. His mother, by all appearances, doted on him. So how could he be afraid of not being loved?

Parents are not perfect. There is no doubt Elvis was everything to Gladys. She did the best she could with her limited resources, but because she overprotected him—loved him as the saying goes, "not too wisely but too well"—Elvis may have thought he had to live his life to please her. He may have felt that Gladys's love never fully respected his individuality. Was he loved for himself only? For the ways he was unlike his mother in addition to the ways he resembled her?

I'm not questioning Elvis's love for his mother. He called her every day from the road and never lived apart from her except when he was traveling. But as he grew to manhood, she often accused him of wanting to escape from her. He must have felt guilty for the most natural and psychologically necessary thing in the world: the desire to make his own decisions and to live his own life.

Unfortunately, Gladys seems not to have been able to love Elvis with a parent's unselfish love; a love that understands that its own delight must give way to the child's welfare, which in the end means letting the child become an adult. I'm finding that out now. It's hard for every parent. Gladys loved him so much that Elvis never had the chance to grow up, to mature in a way that would have enabled him to be a responsible adult capable of setting his own boundaries. He remained dependent on her will so long that his own will never fully developed or gained enough strength to apply itself to his greatest challenges. For all his good will, in significant ways, he was a trapped man. For many years, when he looked inside himself for the resources to break out of his destructive behavior patterns, he was lacking.

He needed someone who could love him for himself, for the best in him, and the worst, and, perhaps most importantly, everything that distinguished him as an individual. He needed someone who would love him unconditionally and at the same time *not* put up with the ways in which he could be mean, petulant, "willful," and self-indulgent. Everyone of us needs this, and not one of us can find it in another human being. After all, the other person is only human and needs the same thing, which we certainly can't supply.

Please believe me when I say that I'm not trying to blame Gladys for Elvis's later excesses. He was her only child, and if she overprotected or spoiled him, it is completely understandable. She did the best she could. None of us are perfect. But after her death, a significant influence in Elvis's life was removed, and he seemed lost.

Being Elvis-the-public-image meant Elvis-the-person had particular difficulties finding anything like what he needed in another person. His ability to grow as a person suffered in consequence. Gladys's influence was gone. Elvis's dependency on her left him without significant direction and restraint. He must have been very afraid.

The old maxim suggests that every crisis is also an opportunity. Gladys's death provided Elvis a real opportunity to confront the deepest questions in his life. For one thing, it made his fears all the more real, and when you can identify your underlying fears, you are a long way toward seeing things aright.

Coming out of the army, Elvis feared his fans' desertion. Haunted by his memories of poverty, determined never to go back, never again to experience life-without-dignity, Elvis craved public acceptance on his return. He was particularly pliable, as a result, and followed the Colonel's directions to the letter.

The Colonel and his advisers in Hollywood—the producer, Hal Wallis, and the president of the William Morris Agency—decided while Elvis was soldiering that the entertainer's interests would best be served by using his military stint to reposition him as a mainstream movie star. He would do three pictures a year, and all his recordings and merchandising deals would be spinoffs of these pictures. He would no longer tour. He had to avoid overexposure in the media. So after the release of each picture and its run, a total publicity black-out followed. Now you see him, now you don't.

The first recordings Elvis made after his army stint reflect this policy. "It's Now or Never" and "Are You Lonesome Tonight?" have Elvis sounding like Perry Como or Dean Martin. Elvis's voice matured while he was in the army; his range expanded and his voice's power increased. It moved more easily from high notes to low. Many of Elvis's critics have failed to note how much his voice improved over the years—a development that provides a striking contrast to most rock 'n' rollers.

His first post-army movie was similarly designed to appeal to a family audience. *G.I. Blues* has Elvis doing some Steve Allen-like turns: a hen-pecked husband skit with a bawling baby and providing the Bavarian folk song accompaniment to a puppet show.

Once Elvis saw that his fans were as loyal as ever, he protested against the new music and movies like *G.I. Blues*. He convinced the Colonel to find him a serious role. He played the half-breed son of a white rancher and an Indian woman in *Flaming Star*. The picture has its moments in the first half and then becomes mediocre due to a faulty script. He also played just the kind of James Dean part in *Wild in the Country* that he had longed for: a young rebel confused as to his own motives but determined to find his own way. Tuesday Weld appeared in the picture with him as a siren luring Elvis on to a destruction that he narrowly avoids. Elvis did his best, perhaps trying too hard at times. Unfortunately, both pictures received poor notices and made very little money.

Elvis's next success ended his chance to become a potentially serious actor—something I believe he could have become. *Blue Hawaii* followed and made millions. Hal Wallis and his screenwriter, Hal Kanter, projected Elvis as the son of a Hawaiian pineapple plantation owner. Elvis "rebels" by hitting the beach. He is engaged to a respectable young woman played by Joan Blackman. Dramatic conflict, what there is of it, ensues when a young tourist tries to seduce Elvis away from his intended. He gives her a good spanking and then marries Joan, sailing with his bride across a lagoon to an old missionary chapel for the concluding ceremony.

"*Blue Hawaii,* say what you want, made money, Elvis," you can hear the Colonel saying. But it also typecast Elvis.

Unfortunately, Elvis listened to the Colonel (and Hollywood) and began the series of pictures he characterized as "travelogues." His fans loved them. He appeared as various reincarnations of himself in these, coming onto the screen as a helicopter pilot, a roustabout, a racecar driver, a sailing captain. He stumbles over an incredible assortment of good-looking girls, fixes his attention on one, she puts up enough resistance to get us through the next two reels, and the romantic conclusion saves Elvis from himself and the girl from any ambitions that run counter to motherhood.

Unwilling to suffer any financial losses as an actor, Elvis chose to make these less-than-artistically-but-materially-rewarding pictures. He did not have the self-esteem to handle rejection; not when a type of success was at hand. He did not have what he truly wanted clearly enough in mind to refuse the Colonel's guidance. He felt these failures and his responsibility for them keenly, however much he might have publicly blamed others for his lot. He did a lot of huffing and puffing about the Colonel, almost all of it fully justified, but he never remedied the situation by firing the man, and for that he was finally responsible.

Instead, he sought comfort. Growing up in clannish Tupelo, he wanted to reconstitute the old pattern, with himself at its center. So he hired various relatives, like Vernon's brother, Vester, and his cousin, Gene Smith, who, with his wife, lived for a number of years over the garage at Graceland. His paternal grandmother, Minnie Mae (or Dodger, as he called her), lived, as I've said, at Graceland, too. At one time or another, Elvis also employed his other Smith cousins, Junior, Travis, and Bobby, as well as Patsy Presley and her husband Gi Gi Gambill.

Then there were The Guys, or the Memphis Mafia (as the media called them), or later, and more formally, the TCB crew (for Taking Care of Business). Elvis kept a group of friends around him who worked as personal bodyguards, dressers, drivers, logistical managers, and gofers, and they partied with him after hours. The Guys were part paramilitary unit (his army experience may have inspired Elvis to start thinking of the people around him as "his troops") and part extended family—people he could trust.

Elvis knew some of the guys from high school. Red West was the one who had defended Elvis when some other members of the Humes High football team were about to give Elvis an impromptu haircut in a bathroom. Red and his cousin, Sonny West, worked for my brother for many years, and Red, in particular, was a talented man who actually wrote one of Elvis's hits, "Separate Ways," and became an actor. Marty Lacker also went to Humes High, and rejoined his school friend as an employee in 1961.

George Klein was president of their class at Humes High, and toured with Elvis until Klein became a successful disc jockey just as Elvis went into the army. He often joined up with the guys later on, though. Elvis always remembered George's kindness to him at Humes, when George was popular and Elvis was not.

Lamar Fike, a three-hundred-pound Paul Bunyan type, known as the "great speckled bird" to insiders, simply showed up one day at Graceland in 1957 to offer his services. Elvis met Joe Esposito, as I've said, in the army, and Joe served for many years as his chief lieutenant and accountant. Priscilla was particularly close with Joe's wife, Joanie. Elvis met Charlie Hodge in the service, too. Charlie, besides his other touring functions, played backup guitar and sang a duet with Elvis on "Could I Fall in Love." In concert, he handed Elvis the scarves the entertainer then threw to the audience. Jerry Schilling joined Elvis in 1964 and was particularly gifted at management, as he also proved by managing Billy Joel and The Beach Boys.

These men and others who worked more briefly for Elvis formed a tight, protective circle around him. True friendship cannot be compelled, and it is difficult to trust when given circumstances that imply constraint, especially financial constraint. Considered individually, the men who surrounded Elvis were a much more talented and varied group than anyone has given them credit for. I'm still proud to say I was a member of that company for a time.

Elvis set himself up for his relationships with these men to be much less rewarding than they might have been. He was unable to recognize that relationships have to have boundaries that are mutually respected. If he wanted these men as true friends, then he probably should not have had them on the payroll, or at least he should have given them well-defined roles that could be evaluated with some measure of objectivity.

Elvis constantly tested his men's loyalty, asking them to get up in the middle of the night to go for hamburgers, get a particular store to open for him after hours, or ferry one of his dates home. He put temptation in their way—one Christmas leaving thousand-dollar bills on his bed to see if any of it would disappear—to prove their motives. He paid them wages that kept them dependent on his famous gifts, a situation that made it difficult for them to get away. Most of the guys loved working for Elvis, but they knew that their place on the team could easily be filled by any one of Elvis's thousands of eager fans. We were all very loyal, and as Elvis found out, trustworthy. But knowledge is power. The person who knows who's getting what, and who's not, has the power. Elvis only became stingy when someone expected something from him, an aspect that inspires most to think of his men's greed, when actually they had a right, and they would have been much better off, if they had known clearly what they might expect in the way of compensation. Their wives came to see it that way, and that was the more objective view. Finally, Elvis was jealous of any outside influence in his men's lives—to the point of wanting, in practice, their chief loyalty to be to him.

Of course, we all knew in advance what it was going to be like to work for Elvis, and we still wanted to be there. He just had a charisma that drew people to him. And then there were the other perks that came with the job. And for a long time the night-after-night, year-after-year party Elvis threw kept everyone happy.

Returning from the army, Elvis entered the life of abandon that has filled so many tabloid accounts. He settled into making three pictures a year in Hollywood and began renting houses where the guys and he could camp out. The first was in Bel Air on Perugia Way, an oval-shaped Middle Eastern home with a central patio and garden that once belonged to the Ali Khan. Elvis next moved into a mansion on Bellagio Road modeled after an Italian villa. The Bellagio Road home proved too accessible, and he hopscotched back to Perugia Way before renting another house on Rocca Place. The guys also used a house in Palm Springs as their weekend getaway.

His interest in women went on, almost uninterrupted, throughout the rest of his career. He spent so much time on the road that his serious relationships—his marriage to Priscilla and his subsequent relationship with Linda Thompson—did little more than provide comforting respites. This aspect of Elvis's life used to be much more shocking. Revelations about the private lives of such public figures as John F. Kennedy, sports stars such as Wilt Chamberlain and Magic Johnson, and so many rock stars of the 1960s that it is impossible to name a single example make it clear that—even in the AIDS-plagued '90s—the temptations of fame are enormous. Average people can best imagine how they might behave by examining their own thoughts. What if you could do these things as easily as imagining them? For Elvis virtually nothing stood in the way of his every wish—a freely swinging door stood at the threshold between fantasy and reality. That did not make it right, but putting it this way certainly helps us understand why it happened.

This also helps to explain Elvis's use of prescription drugs. He began to ease off the Dexedrine highs, which kept him on schedule, by taking tranquilizers and barbiturates. He introduced the guys to Dexamyl, Quaalude, Percodan, Demerol, Seconal, Tuinal, Valium, Nembutal, Placidyl, and various codeine compounds. Pharmacology became one of his enthusiasms, and he carried around the standard guide to drugs and their effects, the *Physicians' Desk Reference*. He saw these "medications" as a way to transcend the normal demands of the body for a reasonable schedule and also as a way to deal with his increasing boredom. Although Elvis always insisted that his medications had legitimate purposes because they were prescribed by doctors, he used them from the beginning for purposes other than those for which they were prescribed. His denial about his drug taking was even more adamant than his will to succeed. Perhaps he could not let himself admit that he was his mother's son in this; not an extension of her, as he would have feared putting it to himself, but someone who had inherited her and her relatives' addictive biochemistry and the false pride that led her to coverup and deny her drinking.

Under the influence of drugs, the synthetic cycle of uppers and downers, Elvis became quick tempered and often hostile. He chewed out the guys more and more frequently. If someone displeased him at his parties, he could become physical.

These are the tragic consequences of drug abuse; the incidents that ought to provide ample evidence and more that the user must quit. Elvis, like others in denial, like me when I became a heroin addict, saw these incidents as freak occurrences that happened for one reason or another, never as the inevitable fallout of self-destructive habits.

Elvis rarely apologized for anything, always explaining why he had messed up instead of simply confessing his wrong when he did ask forgiveness. He was too insecure to risk humbling himself where it really counted, one-on-one. He did feel guilty for much of his behavior—he would have been a monster not to, and he was no monster, just very weak in certain ways and at a loss. His famous gifts to the guys—Cadillacs, clothing, jewelry, cash for special medical expenses, and even houses, sometimes—simply came from his innate generosity. Sometimes, though, the gifts expressed his desire to be forgiven and make things right. It wasn't the best way to apologize, since receiving a gift often brings with it a sense of obligation, which keeps the round of who's-in-control going, but Elvis would have been much less a man than he was if he had been oblivious to how much he hurt people at times. He knew. It tore him up. He just didn't know how to stop the roller coaster.

The parties lost their joy for Elvis not too long after they began in the mid 1960s, even though they would continue, off and on, as a ritualized part of his way of living until his death.

He began to look right and left for something more satisfying.

Really falling in love always suggested itself as a possibility. Elvis must have gone through many periods of doubt about his relationship with Priscilla—before, during, and after their marriage. She was at Graceland during these years, and Elvis, while maintaining his long-term commitment to her, let himself entertain other possibilities.

He starred with Ann-Margret in the film *Viva Las Vegas*. He fell in love with his costar and pursued her as he had not pursued any woman in many years. She felt the same way and probably would have committed herself to Elvis if he had sent Priscilla back

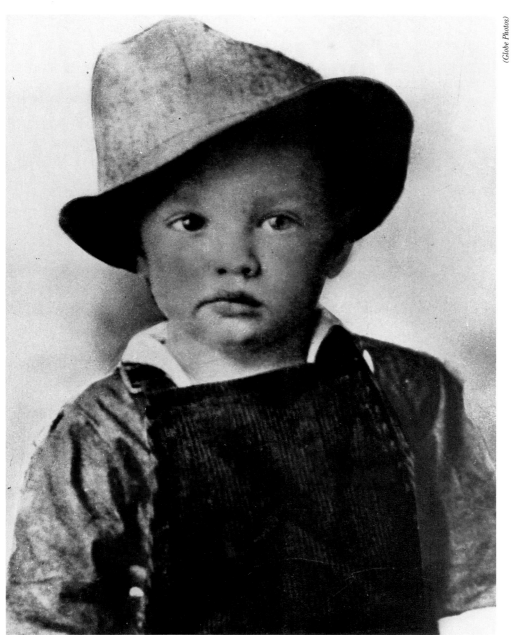

*Elvis at two or three—about the age he remembered starting to "sing" at church. Natural talent usually exhibits itself at a young age.*

*Elvis with his parents outside the Tupelo house. The poverty of his childhood would always remain a factor in the way he related to people and handled money.*

*Elvis at about twelve. He had wanted a bike for his birthday but got a guitar instead. The rest is history.*

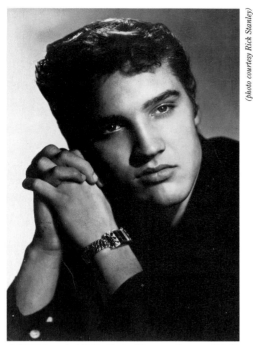

A 1956 tour publicity photo. Thousands were distributed to fans at every concert. The photo is unlike any other Elvis picture, in that it captured a pose that would never again be duplicated.

An early concert. Elvis's band was still small, and his voice was the focal point of the performance. The "Vegas" days were still a long way off.

Tupelo, Mississippi, October 26, 1956. An outdoor concert at the annual fair. His style had come a long way from the day he sang "Old Shep" at the same fair in 1945.

*Elvis, Gladys, and Vernon on the eve of Elvis's induction into the army. Gladys was unaware she was suffering from a life-threatening disease—hepatitis.*

(Globe Photos)

*Elvis at home with Gladys and Vernon just prior to his purchase of Graceland. Never again would he be so accessible to photographers or to the public.*

(UPI/Bettmann)

*"Oh, God, everything I have is gone," Elvis cried. His mother, Gladys, had died that morning of an apparent heart attack. Elvis never completely got over her death.*

*Elvis on the beach in Germany with some fans. Even though Elvis was as popular internationally as he was at home, he never toured outside the United States.*

*Sixteen-year-old Priscilla Beaulieu writes to Elvis. He had just returned to the States for his army discharge. They had been dating for six weeks.*

*(UPI/Bettmann)*

*Elvis and Colonel Tom Parker just after Elvis was discharged from the Army on March 5, 1960. Elvis is giving the colonel his final Army paycheck.*

*(Michael Ochs Archives)*

*(Globe Photos)*

*Elvis on the sets of* Love Me Tender *and* Viva Las Vegas *with Ann-Margret. The difference in the plot and style of these two films symbolizes the ambivalence Elvis felt about his entire film career. The extraordinary financial success of his "musicals" typecast Elvis from then on.*

*Elvis displaying the football trophy his team won in the early sixties. Members of the Memphis Mafia made up the teams.*

*Rick Stanley (behind Elvis) and Charlie Hodge visit the fans at Graceland in 1967. For Rick growing up at Graceland was like being raised at Disney World.*

*Vernon, Dee, Rick Stanley, David Stanley, Elvis, and Billy Stanley in the early '60s. Elvis was brother, friend, and eventually surrogate father to his new siblings.*

*Elvis married Priscilla on May 1, 1967. The fairy tale princess would soon be queen of Graceland.*

*The birth of Lisa Marie, February 1, 1968—exactly nine months to the day following Elvis's marriage to Priscilla.*

*Lisa Marie prepares to take a nap with her daddy. Until the day Elvis died, she was his only consistent source of love and happiness.*

*Elvis and Lisa Marie during the happy days. Although a loving and affectionate father, Elvis would always have difficulty saying no to his daughter.*

*This happy pose in early 1971 contradicts the growing estrangement between Elvis and Priscilla.*

*Elvis and Priscilla leaving the divorce court in 1973. Elvis would never fully recover emotionally.*

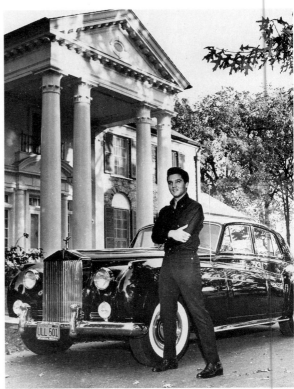

*Fame and Fortune. Elvis at Graceland in the late '60s. His career revitalized, married, and a daughter — he would never be happier.*

*The 1968 NBC Christmas special completed Elvis's musical resurgence that had begun earlier that year with the release of "Guitar Man" and "U.S. Male."*

*Back on tour after being offstage for nearly a decade. Although initially revitalizing Elvis, the physical and emotional strain of touring would be a significant factor in his death.*

*Rick Stanley and Elvis backstage at the Hilton Hotel in Las Vegas in the early '70s. Rick was Elvis's personal assistant and valet for the last seven years of his life.*

*Rick unloading Elvis's most precious possessions while he was on tour—the "black kit" containing his medications and the library of Elvis's religious books.*

*Rick aboard Elvis's plane, the "Lisa Marie," during a 1971 tour. A gold "Taking Care of Business" medallion hangs from his neck—a constant reminder of just how infrequent such moments were.*

*A 1977 snapshot of Elvis playing football on his last vacation in Hawaii. In spite of his weight and physical problems, he continued to enjoy competitive sports, even playing a game of racquetball on the day he died.*

(NBC/Globe Photos)

Aloha from Hawaii via Satellite *played
to the largest television audience in
history. Elvis was able to meet this
challenge, but 1973, the year of his
divorce, signaled the beginning
of his serious chemical dependency.*

(Photo courtesy Rick Stanley)

*Elvis performing on his last tour—March 23 through June 25, 1977. His fans couldn't tell, but Elvis was a very
sick man both physically and emotionally.*

*Rick and Robyn Moye the day after Elvis died. Their forced smiles betray the deep grief they both were feeling.*

*The Stanleys—Christmas 1991. Bethany, Robyn, Rick, and Brittany.*

Each year on August 16, thousands of devoted fans flock to Graceland to commemorate the anniversary of Elvis's death. Their devotion has kept the memory and legacy of Elvis alive.

American Rock Singer 1935–1977
Elvis "officially" enters the mainstream of American cultural heroes with the January 1993 issue of the Elvis stamp.

to her father. Ann-Margret may have been too intent on developing her career for Elvis. When he chose against Ann-Margret for Priscilla, Elvis probably decided, quite consciously, that he—like most men—preferred someone who would be devoted entirely to him. He fell hard for Ann-Margret, though, and he never quite shook his feelings for her.

He also looked to religion for his answers to the searching question that his success had brought with it. His Pentecostal background should have provided firmer footing, a way back to something more nearly like the straight and narrow path. Elvis had several problems with traditional Christianity, though. But mainly he found it almost impossible to obey its precepts. He may have thought that something had to be wrong with a religion that demanded marital fidelity from a man who had women toss their hotel keys at him every night. Or maybe this was the "one great flaw" in his character. I don't know.

But in this, as in so many things, Elvis wanted to find a way to have his cake and eat it, too. On April 30, 1964, Elvis made a new friend when a young man named Larry Geller came to cut his hair. Larry was a devotee of Eastern philosophy and spiritualism. He introduced Elvis to books that sought to coordinate and synthesize the truth of all religions. Larry was particularly attracted to theosophy, the notion that the world was once in possession of an ancient wisdom, known to an enlightened race, the Aryans. The great prophets of the world, the "masters," such as Buddha, Christ, and Mohammed, had conveyed to us fragments of this secret, or esoteric, knowledge. Our task as "adepts" is to reassemble these fragments in our own minds into something resembling the ancient wisdom. To do so brings with it peace, security, and freedom.

One of Elvis's favorite books during this period, *The Impersonal Life,* claims to be a dictation of God's voice through its recorder, Joseph Benner. The book was written in 1917—the heyday of Madame Blavatsky and theosophy. Its form expresses its central idea: that God is immanent in everyone and life flows from identifying the divine within us and following its dictates.

Spiritualism also teaches that true happiness is found in detachment from the world. We transcend our own limited egos, our personalities, by detaching from material possessions, people we love selfishly, and anything we hold onto out of fear. Our personalities are seen as idiosyncratic collections of appetites and fears. By identifying with the divine in each one of us, the *impersonal,* we come into accord with the true spirit that shapes the world. When we are in harmony with the dynamic force of the universe, we find happiness.

*The Impersonal Life* and other such books try to show that their teachings are in accord with Christ's. They see the kind of Christianity in which Elvis was raised as a misinterpretation of its founder's words. The crowd understands Christ to be saying this, but, aha, he's really saying something rather different.

Elvis was not well schooled enough to recognize the central contradiction in the spiritualists' reinterpretation of Christ's message. Many Eastern traditions do see God as impersonal, a collective underlying force rather than an agent with intentions and a will. It's literally and metaphorically impossible to conceive, however, of a more personal image of God than Christ presents—he is, after all, just that, a person. This is Christianity's great peculiarity among other world religions. Christ teaches detachment from our own will, but only in order to follow the will of his Father. That will is largely spelled out, a matter of written principles and the spirit that gives them life, rather than intuitions of an unspecified force.

The attraction that detachment must have held for Elvis must be obvious. He knew how unsatisfying an abundance of riches could be. He must have dearly wanted to escape the toils of his own personality, its binds and contradictions, its trap. T. S. Eliot said that only those who don't have real personalities fail to understand the attraction of escaping the self. His freedom lay in another direction—back toward his own conflicts and the complexity of his past. But Elvis sought to find answers by anesthetizing himself with drugs, and through spiritualism. But the way forward was the way back. His life became impersonal to the degree he failed to live it to the fullest.

Elvis once told Natalie Wood that he had been given a gift from God, and he had to be careful what he did or God would take it away from him. As he became less careful about what he did, he found it convenient to change his conception of God. If God was within him, and he had been "led" to do these things, then he need not worry. Elvis may have well talked himself into this, may have needed to, for an extended period of time. In the end, he knew better. And in the end, I'm convinced, he saw things differently.

His pretensions were great for a while, though. Many people have remarked on Elvis's double-sided nature. The good boy who loved his mother and sang hymns, and the bad boy who was wild and took drugs. In his own mind, there must have been a strong third presence. He was the king of rock 'n' roll. Why had a poor Tupelo boy been given a gift that put all the world at his feet? What did his success mean? What mission had this boy marvel been assigned?

Entertainers make people happy. Gratitude on the part of fans quickly flows into the fans' own need to worship. This need is one of the deep, unrecognized forces of the twentieth century. It's not supposed to exist, so cultural commentators choose not to recognize it whenever possible. So many people worshiped the image Elvis presented, the illusion he produced on stage, that he was left wondering whether his fans did not know better than he did. Maybe he was something more than an individual with his own strengths and weaknesses that inside he always knew himself to be. He wanted to please his fans so much. Maybe he was a kind of spiritual leader. Perhaps he had been sent on a mission to lead the world in a great religious revival. Not of the Pentecostal description, but a revival of the ancient wisdom.

These thoughts led him to attempt spiritual healings. It had him preaching sermons to the girls who attended his Bible studies in his Los Angeles homes. He dabbled with this for years, and his show, in the end, gain in to his fans' need for hero worship.

He gave them his scarves as relics, and he swooped into and out of view by spreading his angelic cape. By the time this image emerged into public view, though, he knew it to be a soul-destroying counterfeit.

# 8

## Comeback

*I* am embarrassed to admit that I was a member of the Presley household for a long time before I became an Elvis fan. Growing up, I liked The Beatles, The Rolling Stones, Led Zeppelin, The Who, and Jimi Hendrix. Although I lived with the man and knew him as my brother, my attitudes toward Elvis were typical of my generation. We did not know him as a rock 'n' roller. We knew him, if at all, as a movie star who sang. At Graceland I watched more of his movies than most of my contemporaries, of course, and I enjoyed the early ones, *Loving You, King Creole,* and *Jailhouse Rock.* It was always a little hard to believe that my stepbrother was up there on the screen. I liked *Blue Hawaii,* too, and *Viva Las Vegas,* but even as a boy I could tell that these films were light entertainment and the songs Elvis sang in them had nothing to do with where rock was going in the 1960s. Sometimes my brothers and I suggested that Elvis sing the new songs. We even had our own fledgling group—a brother act— where we sang such songs as "Hard Day's Night." He would get an embarrassed grin on his face when we'd urge him to record material like this, and say, "Naw, it's not my kind of singin'."

The Beatles came to Graceland once, and they visited with Elvis and the guys in Los Angeles, where Elvis and the Fab Four, after awkward introductions and small talk, finally hit it off. More importantly, he knew the challenge they presented to his position in the music world. He came to despise his own films, his "travelogues" as he called them, and he understood better than anyone how outdated he had become to the younger generation. My generation constituted the vast majority of people who bought records at that time, and Elvis's records, which were mostly soundtracks from his films, declined steadily in sales from 1960 to 1967.

In retrospect, and with the advantage of age, I can see the problem as it probably appeared to Elvis. He understood that the music he helped create and did so much to popularize was developing in new and interesting directions. It was still "mostly gospel," or "gospel mixed with rhythm and blues," but the idiom proved capable of far more elaboration than anyone in the 1950s would have dreamed. "Rubber Soul" and "Sgt. Pepper's Lonely Hearts Club Band" were a long way down the line from "That's All Right Mama." Elvis did not write lyrics or compose music himself, and he did not have the technical interests of musicians like John Lennon and Paul McCartney and Bob Dylan, who interested themselves in how far they could push those three chords that are the basis of the blues. Their Schoenbergian climaxes, baroque brass, sitars, overdubbing, and feedback riffs kept rock growing as a musical form. Elvis became primarily a singer, a creative adapter of others' material, someone who could orchestrate and select the right production values to make a song his own. He was also maturing. Although he had no interest in formal innovation, he needed his songs to expand primarily in terms of their emotional dynamics. His early records are steeped in the trials and tribulations of adolescent romance. But not even the wealth they brought could maintain his interest in them any longer. Nor was he sure he could sing that kind of song again.

So what did he do? He recorded a gospel album, *How Great Thou Art,* which was probably the last strategy a marketing expert might have recommended. Such a move would not have been made by the new groups either. Can you see Paul McCartney releasing an album of traditional pub songs? As an artist and as a great singer, Elvis understood something instinctively that most marketing experts will never understand: His power came from his identity, his being rooted in a particular culture. By making this album he was doing publicly what he always did in private. Before every recording session or public performance Elvis always warmed up with gospel; now he was warming up for a new phase in his career with a gospel album. His impulse to return to his roots in times of crisis had shown itself before. Returning from the service, he recorded *His Hand in Mine* in 1961. Whenever he needed to reestablish his sense of who he was and what he should be about, he went back to the source, gospel.

Elvis recorded *How Great Thou Art* May 25–28, 1966. It was the first time in twenty-eight months that he recorded any non-soundtrack music. It was also the first time that Elvis worked in Nashville with his new RCA producer, Felton Jarvis. A fan and someone who understood Elvis's music and his abilities as an artist, Jarvis over the next few years would be a boon to Elvis's career. He told him he could still cut it and helped him redirect his recordings and reach back for a more soulful sound that connected with his gospel and rhythm and blues roots and, simultaneously, enhanced that sound with an underlayer of mature emotion.

Elvis's decision to record a gospel album, besides providing inspiration for his next steps, had its business side as well. Much of the reason Elvis recorded so much mediocre material resulted from business practices in which Colonel Parker, RCA, Elvis's music publishing company, Hill and Range, and Elvis himself colluded. Hill and Range recruited material for Elvis only from writers who were willing to relinquish half their royalties to Elvis as a legal "coauthor" of the material. This increased Elvis's take on each record by 30 to 50 percent. Early in his career, many writers went along with this arrangement, since having Elvis record their songs increased their chances for a hit astronomically—and half a hit meant a lot more money than all of a flop. Mylon LeFevre's song "Without Him" is a good example. In the 1960s, though, the best writers recorded their own material or could find popular artists who were willing to record their songs on a straightforward basis. Gospel tunes are in the public domain for the most part (or can be recorded at standard rates not subject to dickering), and so Elvis, this once, assured himself that he could sing what he liked. This increased the satisfaction he took in making the record and gave his own producing talents, which were considerable, a chance to assert themselves. This talent was especially evident in his early rock material.

*How Great Thou Art* won a Grammy for best gospel album of the year. It captured the power and versatility of Elvis's mature voice, riding smoothly through the high passages, thumping the bass notes; his voice was so controlled that only once, in the title song, "How Great Thou Art," does he call upon its full crescendoing power.

The album also, it seems to me, begins Elvis's practice of picking songs with lyrics that articulate what he wants said. Most of the selections, such as "Somebody Bigger Than You and I" and "If the Lord Wasn't Walking by My Side" stress God's control over destiny and his compassion and care.

Maybe "Crying in the Chapel" says it best: "You'll search, you'll search / But you'll never find / No way on earth to find peace of mind. / Take your troubles to the chapel / Get down on your knees / Then your burdens will be light / And you'll surely find the way." Those lines must have expressed Elvis's sentiments, or at least, his hopes. He was still in a dark mood and needed to find a new way. Spiritualism still clouded his thinking at this point, but maybe these traditional songs helped him remember the full strength of his Christian tradition.

Before Elvis could sense the power of his bedrock Christian hope, he had to exhaust the dissipation gambit first. He found a ranch just over the Mississippi border from Tennessee one late afternoon as he was tooling around on his Harley-Davidson. The first thing that came into view for him was a fifty-foot, white cross. The cross stood at the edge of a lake, over which arched an oriental bridge. A small farmhouse also marked the 140-acre property.

Elvis investigated and eventually bought the property from the owner. Priscilla and he had lately taken up riding. Elvis began turning the property, renamed the Circle G, into a horse farm. Priscilla saw the place as their own hideaway. Elvis wanted the entire Graceland crowd to go country, and he began buying sporty trucks and mobile homes for the guys, their wives, and families. He bought horses for everyone, too, and as much expensive farm equipment as he could lay his hands on.

The Circle G was great fun. I loved going there and riding the horse Elvis gave me—a pinto like Little Joe Cartwright rode on "Bonanza." His binge spending on the Circle G can only be explained, I'm afraid, by seeing the farm as a huge distraction from his worldly cares. He had started to put his professional house in order with the gospel album, but many aspects of his life remained unattended. Instead of making these (mostly interior) repairs, he put together a Southern fried version of a California commune. Including the guys in the farm scheme upset Elvis's dad, Vernon, who was always concerned about Elvis's extravagant spending. He had blown more than a million dollars and added to his ongoing costs by putting more men on the payroll.

The time came for him to go back to Hollywood to make *Clambake.* A little overweight, frustrated at the prospect of making another "travelogue," he delayed his departure from the Circle G as long as possible. He was also beginning to think seriously about marrying Priscilla, and part of his unhappiness seems attributable to his ambivalence about marriage—a feeling with which most long-term bachelors can identify.

On the eve of *Clambake's* first day of shooting, Elvis got up in the night, went into the bathroom of his house on Rocca Place, and tripped, plunging headfirst into the tub and blacked out. He got himself back to bed. In the morning, when he showed the guys the golfball-sized bump and a doctor came to have a look, Elvis was ordered back to bed. He had suffered a serious concussion.

The Colonel used this incident to regain control of the situation. He screened Elvis from any unwanted visitors and spent most of Elvis's recovery castigating him for his excesses, encouraging his fears about his career, and, in general, reshaping his thoughts to see the Colonel's version of reason. The Colonel cut the guys' salaries, ordered them not to come to Elvis anymore with personal problems, and substituted Joe Esposito for Marty Lacker as crew chief. The Colonel put Marty in charge of special projects, the first being Elvis's wedding. The Colonel also insisted that Elvis stop his experiments in spiritualism and laid down the rule that someone had to be with Elvis and Larry Geller at all times when Larry cut Elvis's hair. In effect, the Colonel prepared the way for Larry's eventual departure—he had Elvis sign off on the "no-spiritualism" provision right away. Not too long after this, indeed, Elvis and Priscilla burned many of his religious books. This delighted Priscilla, since at that time she did not understand the spiritual side of Elvis's nature, begging him, by her own admission, to put his books away.

Most renderings of this crisis make Elvis look like a totally passive victim of the Colonel's browbeating. Elvis used the crisis in his own way, however. If the Colonel wanted concessions from him, he wanted a few things from the Colonel. He wrested more control over his career from the Colonel, finally confronting the pertinent and underlying issues. He would be able to secure better material, with the Hill and Range collateral arrangements weighing less heavily in the choices. The Colonel would begin doing what he could to end the travelogues and move Elvis's career in new directions.

The Colonel told Elvis, by all accounts, that he needed to go ahead and marry Priscilla. Probably reasoning that a wife would moderate Elvis's excesses, the Colonel now saw marriage as a further means of exercising his control. (The Colonel had long been against Elvis marrying on the grounds that marriage would diminish him as a sex symbol.)

Elvis decided to marry Priscilla, although not without having to overcome his pattern of being infatuated with a woman and then thinking twice once he had won her over. Many see this as a sign of terrible emotional immaturity. If it is, then most of the men I've known are emotionally immature. Marriage is a big commitment. It's hard work with new and often stressful responsibilities. Elvis, like any man, must have had his share of doubts.

Nevertheless Elvis made his decision alone—the Colonel had a talk with him, but Elvis decided. To that you can only say that every decision finally comes down to the individual.

The Colonel used the marriage ceremony itself to assert his authority—making the most of the publicity opportunity. Taking care of all the arrangements, he staged it at Las Vegas's Aladdin Hotel on May 1, 1967, in the owner's suite (Milton Prell, an old friend of the Colonel's), with Nevada Supreme Court Justice David Zenoff (another old friend of the Colonel's), presiding. He restricted the guest list, except for Marty Lacker and Joe Esposito, who served as Elvis's two best men. The couple honeymooned in the Bahamas, but only after the Colonel rushed them from the ceremony into a grueling press conference. There's no doubt that Elvis allowed it, and the Colonel simply took care of business.

What Elvis most feared about marriage, its curbs to his own will, contributed substantially to his turnaround in the next two years. Long ago Aristotle said that if a man were able to follow his own wishes absolutely, he would destroy himself within a year. Elvis had just about proved his point, allowing for a time adjustment. The way Priscilla went about asserting her authority, taking over daily operations at Graceland, managing access to Elvis, might not have been appreciated by the guys. Elvis needed someone to stand up to him, though, and Priscilla did. Her strength, even as a fourteen-year-old, had attracted Elvis. He knew, in the depths of his heart, that he needed to be a person among equals, not a demigod among creatures of his will.

As I've already said, it may surprise people to know that Elvis waited until his wedding night to consummate his marriage, but it's true. This testifies to his extreme romanticism, and the importance he attributed to the sacred character of marriage, however much he may have compromised these convictions with others. At least Elvis knew what was right and acknowledged this, even if in a hypocritical fashion.

Nine months to the day, on February 1, 1968, Elvis and Priscilla's daughter, Lisa Marie Presley, was born. Elvis experienced a profound sense of gratitude; the birth of his child put his life into perspective. The night Lisa was born, Elvis called Nancy Sinatra. "I just don't know how I got to be so lucky," he said. "I am so lucky and my little girl is so lucky. But what about all the babies born who don't have anything? Who don't have food!" Then his flooding sentiments carried one of his deep suspicions to the surface: "I should have been a preacher. I should have stayed with the church."

Elvis did not follow up. He knew his calling differed, although he probably felt guilty about this, since anyone who grows up in Pentecostal circles sees the pastorate as a pinnacle. No, the birth of his daughter made Elvis want to acknowledge the true source of his gifts and the wealth they had brought him. He felt grateful to God, and in this clarifying moment he did not confuse the Lord with any "divine self" within. He knew God as an agent quite apart from him, and in most respects, very much unlike him.

Elvis's wonder at God's care, while it contains gratitude, also reveals hints of an un-divine self. Perhaps Elvis's greatest problem might have been that he did not understand grace, and when he did, he did not like it. He had a basic feeling of unworthiness, partly because he, like the rest of us, was selfish and prideful. He did not understand God's reasoning in giving a poor boy from Tupelo, Mississippi, phenomenal gifts as a musician. He could not quite accept that the Lord may have done this simply because he wanted to. It was his good pleasure. Think about that! God decides he's going to raise up one of the last of the last! He's just going to do it. For his own purposes. Maybe only because it pleases him. Then there's Elvis always trying to figure it out, twisting and turning in the bonds of his own ego, rolling toward claiming the gift as his own, reeling toward seeing the gift as an emanation of a polytheistic cosmic consciousness. In effect, Lisa's birth said to him: Ain't no reason you'll ever know, mah boy! You just be grateful. And *enjoy* it.

Most often, this was too much of a mindblower for Elvis to accept. Grace is that way for almost all of us.

I remember when my two daughters were born. I hadn't

realized until then the full extent of the destructive behavior, soul-destroying attitudes, and family-wrecking patterns I had been brought out of. As an adult child of an alcoholic parent, the child of divorce, living always in the shadow of a famous relative and under his tutelage in the fine art of living to excess, I should have ended up dead of an overdose, but because of the grace of a sovereign God, I am a happily married man, with a great ministry trying to help others avoid the same mistakes I made and point them to the Lord. There's nothing finer than that! I'm grateful. I also know how difficult it is to understand the mystery of God's grace. Some would often rather settle for the lie of their own self-sufficiency than see their relationship to God as his creatures so clearly. The birth of a child sheds a glaring light, though.

Elvis went back into the studio in September 1967 (during Priscilla's pregnancy) for a second time with Felton Jarvis. Once again he recorded rhythm and blues tunes reminiscent of his Sun recordings. He cut Jimmy Reed's "Big Boss Man," Tommy Tucker's "High Heeled Sneakers," and Ray Charles's honeysuckle confession, "You Don't Know Me." He also recorded the rocker, "Guitar Man," which became Elvis's biggest hit in a long time. Its January 1968 followup, "U.S. Male," almost a knockoff of the original tune, also scored big. Elvis was coming back, and he was recording vital music.

His movie career exhausted, Elvis needed a new stage. The Colonel put together one of his marketing wonders, a collection of old Christmas tunes and spliced in messages from Elvis that he sold to radio outlets with good results. He decided to let the word "get out" (the Colonel often started business deals by starting rumors) that Elvis might be available for a television special—a form of mass exposure that the Colonel had outlawed since the advent of the three-pictures-a-year strategy with intermittent blackouts. Elvis had not appeared on television since 1960.

The Colonel had in mind a Christmas special à la Perry Como's: Elvis appearing in sumptuous, homey settings, in front of the fireplace by some overstuffed chairs, with a facsimile of the Metropolitan Museum's Christmas tree in one corner. Tasteful.

Expensive looking. A "present" from Elvis to the whole family. The special would continue the policy of broadening Elvis's appeal to the broadest possible audience.

NBC entered into negotiations with the Colonel about the special. The network's ideas for Elvis's first reappearance on television differed radically. They picked Steve Binder to produce the show. Binder had put together the "TAMI Show" in 1965, one of the few television programs ever to capture the true excitement of rock 'n' roll. Everyone from James Brown to Jan and Dean, from Diana Ross to Mick Jagger appeared on that program—perhaps the best snapshot of rock at a particular time ever produced.

Binder liked Elvis's real music; he hated the canned sound-tracks to his movies. He went into the show with one purpose: to re-present Elvis Presley as a vital force in contemporary music. This put him at loggerheads with the Colonel, of course.

Binder played his hand carefully and wisely. In initial meetings about the show's format, he looked past the Colonel's plans to Elvis's own wishes. Much of the reason that this 1968 special, sponsored by Singer Sewing Machines, became a watershed in Elvis's career grows out of Binder's care for Elvis as a person and particularly as an artist. Binder wanted to know who Elvis was. What Elvis wanted. How Elvis saw himself moving on with his career. Almost no one had ever paid attention to Elvis's identity as an artist since Elvis himself had established it. Most people cared about "image," not identity.

In an early meeting, the producer recounted to Elvis how another group, The Association, had refused to record the song "MacArthur Park" since they felt its surrealistic imagery ran counter to their image. He asked Elvis whether he would have made the same decision.

Elvis said he would have jumped at the chance to record "MacArthur Park." "I love that piece of music," he said.

Binder also thought he had a few things to teach Elvis about how the music scene and the world itself had changed. (You can, in fact, see this didactic intention extending itself throughout the special.) When Elvis complained about how his position made him a virtual prisoner, demanded his reclusive way of life, Binder suggested they walk out of his Sunset Strip offices and see what happened.

Binder, Elvis, and a few of the guys stood on a street corner, in front of a striptease joint. No one noticed Elvis, or let on that he did. The star started cutting up, trying to draw people's attention. Still, no reaction. Binder, Elvis, and the entourage went back into the offices. Elvis must have been more frightened than ever that he had lost touch or, worse, become irrelevant. Of course, this test was something of a setup. No one notices anyone in Los Angeles—on principle. Particularly during the hippie days of 1968, everyone would have been too cool to flip out over Elvis Presley on a sidewalk. Elvis's antics then ensured his dismissal. Someone clowning on a Sunset Strip sidewalk was likely to be tripping and to be avoided at all costs. If Elvis had appeared on a street corner in almost any other city in America, he would have been mobbed.

Binder and the Colonel fought over the format of the program to the last. Eventually Binder prevailed, although the Colonel did manage to deny him any royalties as the producer of the soundtrack album. The producer's performance, itself, though, should be seen as more a mixed bag than a grand slam home run. For instance, Binder gave the show its own logo, Elvis spelled out in red neon. An idea that works. Soon after the opening, a tight shot of Elvis singing, "If you're looking for trouble, you've come to the right place," we see the logo with one hundred guitar players or one hundred dancers pantomiming playing behind Elvis. Real showbiz stuff.

But Binder did not quite pay enough attention to Elvis. He had his own bright ideas about who Elvis should be, some of which worked and some of which didn't. In the end the best thing he did was to give Elvis a chance to perform again before an audience.

The best segments of the show come when Elvis, in a full-length black leather costume—Marlon Brando's jacket on top of

Jim Morrison's britches—stands in a ring, surrounded by his audience and . . . sings. Just that. He stalks around the ring between numbers. The music is piped in and takes hold. He starts gyrating once again to the beat. He plays to the audience, working the crowd by appealing to one young woman and then another, who grow gratifyingly hysterical. He looks up and out toward a brighter day, before kneeling as if supplicating the higher powers or at least the woman of his dreams. His voice sounds better than ever. At thirty-three, he even looks better, his face lean and fine edged with experience. He's not quite so friendly; a little more seriously dangerous now.

Binder also put Elvis in a ring with his old guitarist, Scotty Moore, his drummer; D. J. Fontana; Alan Fortas on tambourine; and Charlie Hodge, who played rhythm guitar. Elvis was supposed to reminisce about starting out with Scotty and D.J. and get cooking in the kind of informal backstage jam session that Elvis so often initiated. Binder misjudged Elvis's ability, at least at this point in his career, to relax before the television cameras, even in an intimate setting with a party-sized audience. As he sings "That's All Right," "Lawdy, Lawdy, Miss Clawdy," and "One Night with You," he's looking around most of the time for a way to *perform*. He's only really comfortable when the numbers get cranked up and he's driving with them. The segment shows that Elvis was freed by the music to be something in public that he never really was in private—confident. His role as an entertainer took him out of his own private doubts and insecurities and liberated his powers.

One affecting moment in the production numbers comes through the repetitions of the "Guitar Man" lyrics. The last time Elvis sings these lyrics he's before the real audience again, his true and best venue. "Well, came a long way from the car wash," he sings, "Right to where I said I'd get / Now that I'm here I know for sure / I really ain't got there yet / So I think I'll start all over / Sling my guitar over my back / I'm gonna get myself back on the track / and never ever gonna look back / I'll never be more than what I am / and wouldn't you know, I'm a swingin' little guitar man." Then, as he walks off, he adds, "Take it home son, take it home." It's as if Binder wanted to pound home the truth that Elvis's true identity rested in his music, and he, in his final throw-away line, acknowledges that he's gotten the message, he's come back home. Vernon said he never knew a guitar player worth a damn. But Elvis finally left all his movie star ambitions behind and accepted the role without any more hesitations or pretensions.

Elvis closed the show dressed in a white suit, singing "If I Can Dream." Binder wanted Elvis to make a "concerned" political statement, something, perhaps, about the Vietnam War, the division between the generations. But the Colonel always kept Elvis strictly away from politics. Elvis's own political sentiments might have curled Binder's hair, if he had in fact voiced them. "If I Can Dream," written expressly for this epilogue to the show, turned out to be a secularist anthem, with enough overtones of concern and, as they used to say, "relevance" to complete Elvis's updating. It was written by the special's choral director, Earl Brown. The soul in it released Elvis's power, though, in a memorable finale.

"If I Can Dream" became an immediate hit, and the soundtrack of the special shipped gold. Elvis was back.

He liked working with the special's full range of instrumentation. When he went back into the studio, he determined that he deserved to make a real record with as many resources as the producers and arrangers of the special commanded.

In mid-January of 1969 Elvis went into the Memphis studios of American Recording. American had hot engineers, producers, and an emerging house band, all of whom had taken Elvis's "Memphis Sound" and developed it, making it now the "Stax/Volt" sound. The studio band was led by Tommy Cogbill, a bassist.

In six days in January and an additional five days in February, Elvis and the American Recording band cut the greatest records of Elvis's mature years. He recorded "In the Ghetto," "Kentucky Rain," and the classic, "Suspicious Minds." The albums that came out of these sessions, *From Elvis in Memphis,* and the studio disc of *From Memphis to Vegas/From Vegas to Memphis* set, are probably the best records of Elvis's career. They are the only ones, apart from the gospel records, that approach what used to be called in the '60s "concept albums." These releases have an internal logic, one song flows into the next, and the lyrics present a consistent picture of a mature man in his adult struggles.

"In the Ghetto" might be received as liberal hand wringing, except for Elvis's genuine background in the Tupelo and Memphis ghettos and his sincere integrationist views. (He told the guys what was what on that score when Martin Luther King, Jr. was assassinated, decreeing that mourning and nothing else was the order of the day.) "Kentucky Rain" has a gorgeous sound. It has the voluptuous, gothic, and guilt-ridden elements so prevalent in Southern art. It's like William Faulkner set to music.

"Suspicious Minds" shows Elvis at his mature best. From its opening line, "We're caught in a trap," we move effortlessly through a painful and bewildering landscape of lost love. The power of Elvis's voice builds without ever becoming showy. It's a heartfelt lament, true sentiment all the way. It's a dark song, a song of gathering, almost claustrophobic darkness. Even in Elvis's moment of triumph he seemed to sense what was ahead.

# 9

## The Ceremony Begins

$\mathcal{E}$ lvis went into the 1968 special expressing "sheer terror" at performing before a live audience again. But the sessions he taped in front of the three separate studio audiences invigorated him, and made him determined to go on the road again. His money-making power in Hollywood had declined to the point that Colonel Parker saw the wisdom of launching Elvis Presley once again as a live act.

Before the concert, actually, Alex Shoogey, the general manager of the soon-to-be-opened International Hotel in Las Vegas, approached Parker about Elvis's opening the hotel's palatial showroom. Shoogey, as he tells it, was not all that impressed with the television special; he did not think, at least, that Elvis looked like a Vegas act. The Colonel pressed forward with the deal, though, and booked Elvis into the hotel for a four-week engagement, two shows a night. The figures Shoofey and the Colonel agreed on are variously reported. Elvis himself probably collected $100,000 a week. The whole deal may well have been worth the million dollars that is also reported. The Colonel worked out a host of side arrangements for the band, the staff, and himself. Among others things, he soon negotiated free year-round room and board for himself and a ruinous credit line in the casino.

The Colonel wisely kept Elvis away from appearing as the International's first act. That duty went to Barbra Streisand, and her sophisticated one-woman performances delighted the critics, and although I thoroughly enjoyed it, much of the Vegas crowd was unenthusiastic. They liked big productions in Vegas, singing and dancing, the old Follies-Bergère—Ziegfield—Great-White-Way razzmatazz.

Elvis bombed at the Flamingo Hotel himself in 1956. He approached this new engagement wearily. It gave him more of the opportunity you can see him searching for in the '68 special to redefine himself—rather than having others define him—as an entertainer. Elvis was shrewd about recognizing the expectations of his audiences, to the extent of picking up on their unconscious desires as well as their express wishes. He knew that he would be appearing before the leisure suit crowd who liked big, boffo productions. Die-hard rock 'n' roll fans would come, too. The crowds would be laced with the hippie children of the leisure suit crowd who would come to see if Elvis had anything for them as well. How could he meet these expectations? How could he do so and at the same time find a style that fitted him as a thirty-four-year-old man?

The Colonel envisioned him getting up on the stage with a five-piece rock band. But Elvis had his own ideas, and this time he insisted on them from first to last. He combined everything he had ever learned about performing, from his days attending the all-night sings in Memphis to the lessons of the television special and his latest recordings at American. He assembled a top-flight band led by guitarist James Burton and backed by the drumming of Ronnie Tutt. Jerry Sheff played bass, Glen O. Hardin keyboards, and guitarists/vocalists John Wilkinson and Charlie Hodge filled out the sound.

Elvis did not want to sing solo like Streisand, he wanted to be lead voice of an ensemble, to echo, if distantly, the gospel quartet setup. So he engaged The Imperials, a pop gospel quartet, and The Sweet Inspirations, a black female soul trio. (Later, J. D. Sumner and The Stamps replaced The Imperials, and Voice substituted for The Sweet Inspirations.)

He also stationed a thirty-five-piece symphonic orchestra in the pits directed by Joe Guercio. Some fifty musicians appeared with Elvis. He knew what he needed to impress the Vegas crowds and to please himself. He wanted to enjoy his performances as much as possible, and working with these outstanding musicians gave him a constant lift.

Elvis always had to move to the music, but he did not feel like jittering and jiving so much anymore. For years he had trained to learn the martial art of karate. One bit in the television special had him pantomiming karate moves against a series of attackers like Bruce Lee, and he picked up on the choreographic possibilities of his karate moves. He would move with the stalking, pantherlike fluidity of a karate master, and he would accentuate the drive of his songs' lyrics by flashing karate punches and kicks. He even decided to wear modified karate uniforms, having Bill Bellew make up *gis* in black mohair. (The *gis* transformed into his white pearl-and-rhinestone-studded jumpsuits; sometimes with open-collared tunics embroidered with Aztec designs.)

The act encompassed a lifetime of preparation and bound it up in a style that expressed where he had come from, where he had been, and then, crucially, his final aspirations. It worked well, and his audiences would show this.

In the spring and early summer of 1969, Elvis assembled the crew at Graceland and the band in Los Angeles. Then he took the family on a two-week vacation to Hawaii. Priscilla, Vernon, Dee, my brothers, and I all went to join him at the Hawaiian Hilton Village.

I watched Elvis continue his preparations, dieting, working out, soaking up the sun by the pool to add a tan luster. I could see how much this meant to him. He became irritable, didn't quite know what to do with himself. He left us a week early to go to Vegas and check out the scene.

Elvis probably saw Tom Jones's show there. Some writers have given Tom Jones a lot of credit for showing Elvis how to wow the Vegas crowds. Elvis did become friends with Tom Jones during this time and respected him enormously as an entertainer. Jones probably did show him that the older Vegas crowds could be whipped into an erotic frenzy just like the teeny boppers Elvis had appealed to in the late 1950s. The television special shows

Elvis striking poses at the end of songs and leaning back into songs similar to Jones, but mostly, it seems, Jones provided encouragement and a few helpful hints.

When I flew with my family to Las Vegas for the opening, I found a town buzzing with excitement and anticipation. There were posters and billboards everywhere proclaiming Elvis's performances. His songs blasted from every radio. The Colonel's blitzkrieg media announcements virtually rang off the walls. Elvis! Elvis! Now! Now! International Hotel! Elvis's name confronted us at every turn, from t-shirts on pretty girls to the huge neon sign at the International.

People started recognizing Billy, David, and me as Elvis's stepbrothers. As an impressionable, sixteen-year-old, I gloried in the attention—much to my mother's dismay.

On July 26, 1969, when the lights finally dimmed for the first show and we were escorted to our booth in front of the stage, I didn't think I could endure the warm-up acts before Elvis appeared. At last the gold lamé curtain dropped and rose and Elvis, without any introduction, walked out onto the stage in his black karate *gi*. The audience rose to its feet, some people climbed up on their chairs, and the huge room filled with screams and applause.

Elvis belted out, "One for the money!" And the band went bah-duh bum. Elvis sang, "Two for the show / Three to get ready, and go cat, go!" From that moment the night flew away in a powerful exhibition of showmanship and an equally powerful, if not overwhelming, audience response.

I was mesmerized by Elvis's hypnotic ability to single us out and pull us into his song. He was so magnificent even my mom was beside herself, jumping up and down, lost in his ability to make music.

I have to tell you that I had never quite "gotten it" until that night: why people made so much over Elvis. That night I felt it. A power that lifted you up and made you think anything was possible—that gave you hope, consoled your loneliness, and inspired you to start again.

After the show, we went backstage. I saw Colonel Parker come in and lift Elvis off the ground in a bear hug. He kept saying, "My boy!" with such pride. That was a shocker since Elvis and the Colonel had so little personal contact, and they never embraced. That was the first time I had ever seen them even touch. Other stars flocked around telling Elvis how great he was, too.

In her review of the shows, Ellen Willis of *The New Yorker* said, "the next night he was loose enough to fool around with the audience, accepting handkerchiefs to mop his forehead and reaching out his hands to women in the front row. During both performances there was a fair amount of sighing and screaming, but it was more in fun than in ecstasy. It was the ritual that counted."

I would not have known what she was talking about at the time. I was experiencing the power of that ritual too much to understand its character. In retrospect, though, some fifteen years after Elvis's death, and after lots of experience with rituals, I think I can see what she meant and maybe a bit more. The emotions his singing inspired—hope, consolation, love—paralleled religious ones. Into this mix he also introduced power. In church, the minister is in an influential position. And while he is ultimately trying to point to someone beyond himself, to inspire the worship of the Lord, sometimes that adoration gets misdirected his way. In Elvis's case, the emotions he inspired sometimes touched his fans' powerful needs to worship. Since the most logical object to idolize was the cause of these powerful emotions, that need was fulfilled in Elvis; he stood as the unwitting leader of this ceremony and as its object. No wonder people wanted to tear him apart, to take away scraps of his clothing, a kiss, or any encounter.

The reaction he inspired always largely mystified Elvis. If he understood it, he understood it instinctively for the most part. He understood how to use it to move his audiences. So he added elements to his act like giving away his sweat-stained scarves. He added entering the stage to the music of "Also Sprach Zarathustra," a Wagnerian piece celebrating Nietzsche's Superman figure and recently popularized in Stanley Kubrick's *2001:*

*A Space Odyssey.* He added the capes and spread his arms in them like Superman.

With his background in the church and his knowledge of the Scriptures, he also must have understood, to some degree, that when people crave to touch you and journey to see you with hopes that merely being in your presence will bring about some kind of happiness in their lives, then you are being worshiped; people can unconsciously deify you. Elvis tried to think through these reactions and rationalize them in several ways. But the utter distance between who he was really and what people felt about him confused him. He never wanted to be venerated or even refered to as the king. Trouble was, in the latter part of his career, as he toured the country he was aware (as we all were) that many of his fans were reserving a godlike adoration for him alone.

Veneration carries a pretty heavy responsibility for anyone. He'd met so many of his fans' emotional needs. Living with that could kill anyone. He tried to play up to these expectations and he ended up finding it impossible. He was totally devoted to his fans. He loved them enough to give them everything he had— even when he was physically unable to do so.

I loved my stepbrother, miss him, and cherish his memory. But I have never looked to him as a god-figure, lately risen from death, who chooses to haunt convenience stores in Minnesota or fast-food restaurants in Michigan. That would be the last thing he would want, and I will not have him stolen from me twice as a brother by those whose broken hearts and unmet needs are so great that they cannot control their imaginations.

His humanity became much too real soon after his first Vegas show and the institution of his new work routine, which called for him to make biannual appearances in Las Vegas, in August and February, and to tour through large towns and small for most of the rest of the year.

I had always wanted nothing more than to join Elvis's gang as one of the guys. He knew this and soon asked me to join the Taking Care of Business crew. Elvis always felt he could trust me more than others. We needed and understood each other. So, as some of the older guys wanted to stay home more, Elvis brought first me and later my brothers onto his staff.

My mother hit the roof when she first heard of the idea, of course. I hadn't even finished high school yet!

Elvis sat down with her and promised he would supply all my needs. He would teach me things about life that couldn't be found in a classroom, and he would even hire a tutor.

Vernon knew of my sense of loyalty and wanted to see me helping his son, and he never had much respect for traditional education anyway. Elvis and Daddy persuaded my mother that I could begin a rewarding professional life immediately.

The first time I boarded Elvis's plane with the guys, he let me know that he would be my tutor. He told me that whatever went on was between the guys. It had always been that way, and it would remain that way.

I worked hard, though. I was often on call twenty-four hours a day; at first I did anything that needed doing, but before too long I was Elvis's personal aide and what you might call his communications director. Before long I was handling all the calls coming in to him and going out. I was like a president's appointment secretary— the one who knows who gets access and who doesn't, and who might, and on what terms they might. Certain people had immediate access: Colonel Parker, Priscilla, Joe, Jerry, Charlie, and "Dr. Nick" (Dr. George Nichopoulos), his physician. Although he didn't talk on the phone much, people from all over the country called to request tickets and backstage meetings.

Besides helping with these arrangements, I helped him dress, dried his hair, put towels on his throat to protect his voice. When my brother Billy came on tour, he supervised his meals, seeing to it that the chef in each hotel prepared Elvis's Spanish omelets to his own recipe and making sure that the hotel burned his nightly steak. Billy made sure Elvis had plenty of Mountain Valley water, took care of his wardrobe, made sure that the hotel rooms were ice cold and stationed humidifiers in Elvis's suite to protect his voice. Together we put foil over the windows in Elvis's hotel so that he could continue his night-into-day and day-into-night schedule. When my brother David came on tour, he helped out mostly with security. Elvis enjoyed Billy's sense of humor, his capacity to be embarrassed and kidded, and his eagerness to perform whatever was asked of him. He also liked the sense of quiet strength that David carried with him.

I also collected prescriptions from Dr. Nick and Elvis's other suppliers. Many times these prescriptions were written in the names of the crew, but a lot went straight to Elvis. When I first came on board, I was amazed at all the pressures on Elvis. I found my responsibilities nearly overwhelming and could not imagine dealing with the pressures Elvis was under. It made sense to me that Elvis needed medications to calm down after a show. It also made sense that he would often need help in controlling his sleeping habits and energy levels given our inhuman touring schedule. Changing the schedule itself never occurred to anyone—there was money to be made.

In February 1972, Priscilla's relationship with Mike Stone became known when she told Elvis she was leaving him. They talked and Priscilla informed Elvis that she had finally grown up. Karate, her dancing lessons, and being out in the world on her own had convinced her that she needed to live her own life. She said Elvis had not lost her to another man but to a life of her own.

Elvis begged her to stay and promised to make everything right. Priscilla had heard these things many times before. By her own admission she early adopted a policy of not asking too many questions. But she had recently dropped in on Elvis in his Palm Springs hideaway and discovered letters from fans who had recently been to one of the guys' parties. She could no longer deny the evidence she had on every hand that Elvis wanted her to remain the mistress of Graceland, the mother of his child, and stay out of the rest of his life. She had taken all that she could.

Elvis reacted with predictable anger to this turn of events. He went through wild cycles of depression and rage. And everyone agrees that Elvis's drug intake accelerated unbelievably during this period. He simply could not find enough anesthetic to ease his pain and guilt.

To their credit, Priscilla, Elvis, and Lisa Marie's relationship changed very little as a result of the divorce. He saw his daughter just about as much as ever, although at one point, when Priscilla became concerned about Elvis's drug taking, Elvis faced the threat of having his access to Lisa Marie limited. Cilla has always been a great mom.

Obviously, Elvis's pain came from the wound inflicted on his pride. He thought that Priscilla should be content to remain the way he wanted her, his wifely *extension*. She demonstrated that she had a will of her own. Elvis blamed Mike Stone so much because he could not face a world in which his loved ones were free agents who could do as they pleased. That contradicted the pattern of love that he had learned. It made love itself a challenge for which he remained unprepared. He only knew how to function in the world as "the king," orchestrating those around him as extensions of his will. He did not know how to function in a relationship of mutual obligations and responsibilities; how to take care of himself, nurture but not control his spouse, and accept the inevitable riskiness of the other's love being a free choice. He did not understand that love cannot exist without freedom for both parties and license for neither.

Psychological pain, like a thistled seedpod, always contains the information we need to grow, however prickly its exterior. The breakup (like Gladys's death) provided a great opportunity for Elvis to reorient his relationships, to try again and in a different way. Unfortunately, he simply anesthetized the pain until it diminished enough for him to return to the old routine.

Elvis soon met a local girl, a stunner, Miss Tennessee of 1972, Linda Thompson. Linda helped bring Elvis out of his black mood. Linda may well have been the one woman in Elvis's life whose temperament best suited his needs. She could adapt in almost any situation.

While I was on tour with Elvis, I continued a friendship, mostly by phone, with a young woman I had met in my first years of high school. Her name was Robyn Moye. In Memphis we had high school fraternities and sororities. While still in high school, I was asked to be the "big brother" of one of the sororities. I went to one of their parties and saw a blonde, vivacious cheerleader with clear eyes and that tanned, California-girl look. I asked about her and found out she was that rarity, a young woman with real principles. She was just the kind of "good Christian girl" my mother had always advised me I needed. I might have told you at the time that the notion of a "good Christian girl" was a complete turnoff. When I met Robyn I found out I much preferred everything I would have described as "uncool."

Later, while on the road with Elvis, I kept calling her. She was always happy, her voice full of enthusiasm. She was easy for me to talk to. We developed a close friendship.

When I cruised back into Memphis, I tried to impress her. She asked me to come to a basketball game where she would be a cheerleader. I drove up in my white Trans Am, dressed to kill in gold chains and a silk shirt. I looked a sight strutting over to the bleachers, making my entrance fashionably late, drawing Robyn's and the crowd's attention.

Another time I asked her to a concert Elvis was giving in Memphis. I took Robyn backstage to meet Elvis, and from the way he looked at her, I could see he was thinking: "Way to go little brother!"

She started asking me to go to church with her. I told her no. I wanted no part of church as I knew it in my legalistic church background.

That did not stop Robyn from talking about her faith. She was a "good Christian girl" all right. But I didn't mind. She did not talk about church so much as she did about Jesus. He was real to her; she acted as if he were right with her all the time. I listened. I had met a lot of people who spoke about their "Lord" and then acted like everybody else. She was different. She believed in and kept to the straight-and-narrow path.

Robyn did let me know how much she cared for me. In retrospect, I'm not sure why. She was always there for me, as a comforting voice on the phone, as a friend when I was in town. I told her only selected portions of the life I was leading: the difficulties and loneliness of life on the road, but not all the drug use. I know now that she understood much of what I did not say—she was not that naive. By God's grace, she saw something in me that I hardly knew existed and was too stupid to value. She knew that I threw myself into everything headfirst—all or nothing—and what an incredible Christian I would make if that force was channeled in the right direction.

Elvis had his lifeline in gospel music. Robyn provided a similar tether, even as I went way beyond what I thought must be the point of no return. Soon my stepbrother and I would strain every fiber to the breaking point.

# 10

## The End of Lonely Street

*E*lvis never received any good advice about money. Colonel Parker wanted to avoid any inquiries into his life by the government, and so he *overpaid* his taxes. He drilled it into Elvis's head that many performers had been ruined by failing to pay the IRS. So Elvis never sheltered any of his income. He gave the government its percentage right off the top. He did not sock any money away, either—his investment portfolio seems to have included one ill-advised scheme to build racquetball courts. By 1975 he had made a hundred million dollars and had almost nothing to show for it. A combination of his extravagant lifestyle and lavish generosity were mostly to blame.

One deal the Colonel made shows more clearly than any other the deterioration of Elvis's financial position. In March 1973, the Colonel sold Elvis's entire record catalog outright to RCA. Elvis received $5.4 million, plus a $500,000 guarantee against royalties for seven years. This was a lot of money, but it was nothing compared to what these records would make over the long term.

The Colonel's shortsighted, self-interested mismanagement is clear to us today. In 1980, the probate court reviewing Elvis's estate took the estate's management away from the Colonel and instructed Memphis attorney Blanchard Tual to investigate whether Colonel Parker had consistently acted in his client's best interest. Tual's negative report led the court to stop all payments to the Colonel. The estate then sued RCA and him for the return of Elvis's royalties and secured these in an out-of-court settlement that granted Colonel Parker one last Elvis payday. Reports have it that the Colonel was given 50 percent of all record royalties earned before September 1982 and $2 million in cash from RCA. At the time of the suit, Elvis's estate was worth no more than $5 million or $6 million. Proper money management has seen its value increase to more than $75 million today.

In the 1970s the Colonel spoke of riding his horse (meaning Elvis) for all he was worth. Elvis's biyearly engagements in Las Vegas became part of a year-round concert schedule. In the six years that Elvis performed in Las Vegas, Elvis and the crew had only seven weeks of rest. Events like Elvis's triumphant shows in New York in 1972 and the satellite show from Hawaii in 1973 provided challenges that spurred Elvis to gather his energies and rise to new heights. (He was always up for a new challenge.) But the constant touring wore him down. Additionally, his drugs, which he used to maintain this schedule, took far more out of him than he realized. Elvis went everywhere, even into indoor arenas like the Astrodome and the Silverdome where the sound echoed so badly that he and the band hardly knew where they were in a song. At the Silverdome, Elvis's pants split, an embarrassment that he took with good humor; he saw the whole evening as a comedy of errors, if a lucrative one.

Mostly, Elvis visited the Jacksonvilles, Dubuques, and Scrantons that he had always played. Substantial offers came in from Europe and Japan, but the Colonel continued his policy of not departing from the States. The satellite show from Hawaii attracted a 98 percent share of the audience; still, the Colonel kept up the breakneck pace. I followed along on that never-ending route, that jet-set treadmill, and I can tell you that we kept up a killing pace.

I watched Elvis go through his preconcert jitters. He was always afraid; he never got over the butterflies and sometimes had stage fright; panic would hit him in the middle of a performance, which would cause him to either forget some lyrics or lose his place. Beforehand, when I would hand him his cup of honey-laced tea and massage his neck, and afterward when I would put towels around his neck and run with him to the waiting limousine ("Elvis has left the building!" became one of the most famous lines in show business), I saw how much he gave his fans. Most people say, how much of *himself* he gave to his fans.

He never really gave *himself* to the fans, as he well knew. They never saw the "real" Elvis; they experienced the "image." He performed. He produced not only songs but an illusion of a man whose power, as seen in its effect on his audiences, seemed limitless. He understood how much his fans were hooked on that image. That powerful image! If Elvis as a person could wield such power, could possess such magic, then maybe, just maybe, they might be able to capture the same thing someday. Elvis looked like someone who was exempt from the darkest insecurities we have about ourselves; many times we are not loved for who we really are, but who others think we are. What a colossal irony! Elvis felt like that almost constantly. He fought so hard against that feeling that he persuaded a good part of the world to believe in the image of self-sufficiency and power he presented. Underneath, he never bought it himself. The shy, insecure little boy was always just below the surface.

What came to terrorize him was the knowledge that what he appeared to be, this godlike image, meant so much to his fans. He depended on them for the wealth and fame to which he had grown so attached. What if they found out it was all done simply to meet their expectations? Every night, as he went on stage, he reexperienced what he had said soon after fame first came to him: "An image is a hard thing to live up to." He did give a lot. He gave his every energy to producing the image that his fans craved.

For my part, I think he came to see his image as a trap. It kept him, he thought, from being the person he really was.

He never really tried to escape the trap, though. His childhood taught him that he would only receive love if he pleased people, if he served as the projection of their dreams, their own egos. Through his career he learned what pleased his fans, not just the songs themselves and his talents as a singer, but this image of Elvis as a superhero. In a sense, his fans became everything to him. They became his last family. In his final role he played the favored son, his fans' dreams fulfilled, whom he served as hero and idol—but strictly according to their dictates. Instead of being in control of his own life, Elvis made himself a slave to his fans. But he was a willing slave. They needed each other. And if in the end it can be said that Elvis literally worked himself to death for his fans, at least in his death he obliged the greatest fantasy his music ever promised, that age is a state of mind and dreamers are forever young.

But that legacy was yet to be, and until then he found that this life increasingly lacked purpose. How could he not? He was living out a lie on a colossal scale. After Gladys's death and Priscilla's desertion, the guy's esteem was rendered worthless, and so he looked to his fans as his last source of love. But he never had an equal, no one who could look him in the eye and tell him what was what. He was never under anyone's authority. There were no boundaries in his life. Some friends tried to talk to him from time to time, but Elvis was too hooked on his image to allow for that much mutuality. In these instances, he chose to believe the lie.

You get depressed when you do something you think is absolutely necessary but find increasingly unfulfilling. In his last years of touring, Elvis suffered all the classic signs of depression: lack of energy, sleeplessness, sudden eruptions of temper, and an almost unremitting inability to enjoy himself. His drugs both masked these signs and made them worse. Because of this he no longer enjoyed the life he had labored so hard and so long to make possible.

New prospects sometimes piqued his interest and gave him a renewed hope. Barbra Streisand approached Elvis about appearing in her remake of *A Star Is Born*. She wanted him for her leading man. Elvis loved the idea and prepared to play the part almost immediately. Colonel Parker frittered away the chance because he would not let Elvis receive anything but top billing.

This enraged Elvis. Even when he tried to reach out and escape his image, his manager kept him firmly locked within that suffocating cocoon.

Elvis did play other "roles" in life. Behind the scenes, he adopted the role of undercover narcotics agent, going so far as to visit President Nixon in order to obtain a Drug Enforcement Agency badge. He played at being "Dirty Harry," and he had his "Superfly" costumes. His enthusiasms—collecting police badges, guns, slot-cars, racquetball, and karate—let him drop the burden of "being Elvis" for a while. His need for these distractions tells us what a burden "being Elvis" really was, and the fact that he was still a little boy in many ways.

His use of prescription drugs clinches the case about the burden of being Elvis. I think of the Randy Newman line: "It takes a whole lot of medicine / to make me believe that I'm somebody else." Elvis became the most publicized prescription drug abuser in modern history. A fact that has been commented upon endlessly. We all knew something was terribly wrong. One detail probably suffices to explain how bad it was. I often brought him his sleeping medications. Toward the end of his life, his "drug protocol," his usual dosages, called for him to take three separate "attacks" or packages of powerful tranquilizers, opium-based drugs, and barbiturates, some orally and some by injection.

That's crazy. But those of us around him at the time were so crazy that we hardly knew what to do.

Elvis did have his chances. Beginning in late 1974, Elvis went into the hospital, usually Memphis Baptist Hospital, to dry out. Usually these hospitalizations were attributed to his other health problems. He suffered from glaucoma, hypoglycemia, an enlarged heart, high blood pressure, liver disease, a bad back, and a twisted colon. He really was a physically sick man. But he often exaggerated his need of pain medications on these conditions. Most of his health problems, though, resulted from his drug abuse.

Although Alcoholics Anonymous was certainly in existence at that time, the medical community knew much less about alcohol and drug abuse than it does now. Physicians did not understand the right measures to take. Just monitoring the medication was not enough, and Elvis's personal physicians were in his back pocket. New ones who started dealing with this famous patient were quickly charmed by him. They almost always relented from the stern measures they prescribed at first. Elvis did some drying out during his hospital stays, but once out of the hospital, drugs were readily available to him again. No program that he underwent ever addressed the spiritual side of his disease—the one element from which he could have drawn strength. He really did want help.

Ed Hookstraaten, Elvis's Los Angeles attorney, organized, to his credit, the closest thing Elvis ever knew to a true drug intervention—that procedure in which family members and others close to the drug abuser confront him with his behavior. Hookstraaten hired detectives to find out how Elvis obtained his drugs. The detectives confronted these physicians (there were others they had not discovered), and they defended their behavior. Finally, in the late spring of 1976, Hookstraaten discussed a plan with Priscilla to get Elvis into the Scripps Clinic in San Diego for a three- or four-month stay, to be followed by an additional time of recuperation in Hawaii. Priscilla took the plan to Elvis. He would have none of it.

I say this from the standpoint of a fellow addict. I would have done just about anything to get drugs when I was using. Like most people with addictive tendencies, the first time I drank I got blitzed. The summer following my eighth-grade year in school, I was over at a friend's house when he suggested we raid his parents' bar. I thought I was pretty hot stuff and could handle anything. Having heard about the parties Elvis and the guys staged, I was eager to experience "getting wild."

My friend started to fill a small glass for me, and I asked for a larger one. He found a tall, slender glass and filled it with vodka, gin, bourbon, scotch, schnapps, cointreau, Dubonnet, whatever he could find. "This is what you call a mixed drink," he said, wagging his head like a sophisticate.

I downed it. Asked for a second. After the second, I waited for something to happen. I decided that I would feel the effect faster if I ran around the house—got the "medicine" pumping into my system. I took off. Then I *really* took off. This was no mere inebriation. This was spontaneous combustion, the liquid-fuel takeoff of an ICBM. I sailed into a dizzying sky; my mind became a comet following its own light-year loose orbit, rampaging through the cosmic order. I felt more than terrific.

We decided to go to a friend's house to play kickball. By the time we arrived, I couldn't see the ball. Everyone looked and laughed at me, but I could hardly stand up.

We moved the party to another friend's house. He had a pool. I saw the water and felt the urge to plunge in. Following my lead, several others joined me and jumped into the pool.

Then the mothers arrived. We scrambled out and tried to hightail it. I skidded down a hill into a loblolly, a mudhole. My friend and I began covering ourselves with mud.

Suddenly I came to believe I was dying. I informed my friend. He told me to get up and get out of there. He started to walk away. I grabbed his ankle. We accused each other of being responsible for the fix in which we found ourselves, covered with mud and with our parents on the prowl.

I started for home, covered with mud, plastered with it—still plastered out of my mind as well. Sick, boy, and feeling *real* sick.

When I arrived home on shaky legs, I found my mother and a friend in the living room. She asked me to come in so she could introduce me. I croaked out that I had eaten a bad hot dog, felt sick, and headed for my room.

I threw up in the bathroom before she came after me. She found me lying face down on top of what used to be my bedspread. She insisted we go to a doctor, although I begged to stay at home. She told me I was going to be just like my real father—an alcoholic.

The doctor opened my mouth, had me say "ah," and almost retched himself from my breath. "Mrs. Presley, your son is drunk," he said, recovering his composure. "Would you like me to examine him further?" She said she would take it from there.

Why I continued to find alcohol and then drugs attractive remains the mystery that I now share with others afflicted with addictive disorders. Maybe it was an unconscious way of getting attention, or an attempt to be a part of the group. When others perceive a red light, we think, *Go, man, go.*

When I joined the TCB crew on tour with Elvis, I rationalized that I needed speed to keep my energy level up and downers to unwind whenever I had the opportunity. I soon found friends who did drugs—you score and party with the same people, generally.

We checked into hotel rooms and experimented for days on end with various combinations. I was into speedballing, mixing cocaine and heroin together, staying up for days at a time in a racy, numb state.

My drug taking got worse around the time of Elvis and Priscilla's breakup. Within nine months after Elvis and Priscilla's separation, Linda Thompson became a permanent part of the touring scene. This caused dissension among the guys. "No wives" had been the rule, and now Linda assumed both the role of Elvis's wife and his steady traveling companion—a previously unheard-of combination.

One night I came home to the mansion in my regular drug-induced euphoria and interrupted a session of Linda-bashing by the guys. Although I did not feel threatened by her (in fact, I actually liked her), I went along with the biting remarks. In fact, I started shouting about how Elvis should get rid of her. I was buzzing along on the drugs and rising to new heights of invective spurred on by my audience.

Why? Just like Elvis—like you—I wanted to think better of myself. I wanted to be the person in control, the object of everyone's admiration. I wanted to say what's what, to judge, and mete out retribution. Maybe that's saying a lot for a "cut session" among the boys, but envy and hatred are small instances of big and destructive things.

Sadly for me, Linda overheard my little tirade and was very upset.

Elvis called and told me I had blown it. He was going to have to ask me to leave the crew until Linda settled down and things blew over. I was astounded. I couldn't believe he would do this to me over a girl. He could have as many girls as he liked. But I knew from his tone that he meant it.

I hoped he would change his mind, and I timed my departure the next day at a time when I knew he would be having breakfast. Linda was there with him and left the room when I entered. He just looked at me with tears in his eyes and told me to keep in touch. I felt totally abandoned. I walked out of the house feeling empty and rejected.

I went to live at a motel. Instead of seeing drugs as part of my problem, I looked to them for answers they had never supplied. I fell into despair.

I still had enough sense to call Robyn. We met at her parents' house. She looked great, and her being there brought a sense of happiness. I told her about what had happened with Lynda and Elvis. I didn't tell her about the drugs. She told me that her relationship with Christ sustained her when she faced problems.

I said, "I'm just not into that."

She dropped the subject. In her wisdom she understood there's no use talking when someone is unwilling to listen. She stayed by me, and her strength spoke eloquently of her faith through every silence.

Robyn's example should have taught me more. My drug habit continued to grow. I thought about how I would finance it, now that I was off the tour. I even considered dealing. Then a friend of mine told me his solution. He knew a doctor who would write a prescription for synthetic drugs if the patient convinced him he would enter a drug rehabilitation center.

I convinced the doctor. We partied on for several months, taking some of the synthetic drugs, selling others so that we could get a taste of the real thing. I started tying off and mainlining smack. I got so strung out I nearly stopped eating. I was turning my body into a drug-using machine.

We ran out of every drug we could beg or borrow. So I tried filling a counterfeit prescription. I walked into a hospital pharmacy with hair down to my waist, wearing a t-shirt, jeans, and flip-flops. I appeared at the pharmacy counter, a dead-eyed space cadet with needle tracks all over my arms and asked the girl to fill my prescription.

She took one look at me and hit a secret button, alerting security. Even in my whacked-out state I realized she was taking too long and decided to get out of there as quickly as I could. When I turned, I found myself looking down the barrel of a .38 pistol held by one of two policemen. The other one had assumed a prone position, and he was aiming his gun at me, too.

"Hit the floor!" they yelled.

I hit it. They grabbed me and dragged me down the hall to an office. They yelled at me a while and then threw me into the back of their squad car. I watched them question the girl at the counter and my friend who was waiting on me. My friend insisted he thought I was sick and that was the only reason he had come with me. They didn't believe him. They took us both to jail.

That ride to the station was one of the worst experiences of my life. I felt like the biggest low-life.

When we arrived, they took me to an interrogation room and asked my name and address. I watched the shock on their faces as it dawned on them that I was Elvis's stepbrother. Still, they did what they should have done; they booked me and treated me like anyone else.

I was fingerprinted and photographed, and then I was put into a cell with another addict. I later realized they were merciful in choosing my cellmate. Many of the other prisoners were violent. I could hear screams of pain, crying, and fights breaking out down the long line of cells. I heard language even I couldn't believe. Jail came closer to hell than I ever could have imagined.

My cellmate fell asleep, using a roll of toilet paper as his pillow. I felt myself going catatonic, and I crouched down in the corner of the cubicle. I was afraid and couldn't shake the thought of seeing the look of disappointment on Elvis's face.

Sometime later I heard the guard yell out that I had a visitor. I felt excited and afraid at once. I heard footsteps and saw a beam of light approaching. My emotions went up a notch to terror and exhilaration.

Two guards came to my cell and cuffed my hands behind my back. They walked me back down the long hallway and onto an elevator that took us downstairs. I asked where we were going.

"You got a visitor," one guard said. "You deaf?"

When we arrived at the door, the guards stood me with my nose almost against its metal. The door opened, and there stood Elvis.

"This is going to kill your mom," he said quietly. "It's going to wipe her out."

"I know," I said, looking down at the floor. I felt ashamed, embarrassed, and humiliated. There I was standing in front of my big brother, my lifelong hero, with guards around me and my hands cuffed.

He walked closer, put his arms around my neck and hugged me. I will never forget how much I needed that. I knew I had fouled up. He didn't have to rub it in, and he didn't. How I wish I could have returned the favor. When others criticize Elvis and when I see his faults myself, I think of this moment and recognize the great humanity in the man, and wish . . . I wish so much.

"I'm going to take care of this thing," he said. "Don't worry." Then he whispered in my ear, "Why didn't you come to me? If you needed anything, you could have come to me." Drugs weren't considered a problem with Elvis, but just a way to have fun or escape from problems.

Those words were full of comfort. I realize now, though, that while Elvis meant well, his constant effort to "take care of this thing" was part of the problem. What I needed, his money, his fame, and his power could not supply. I had to find what I needed by myself, and this low point in my life should have given me all the incentive I needed.

Elvis's influence on the Memphis Police Department was considerable because he provided financial support for their softball program and their uniforms. And they appreciated his generosity to other organizations and people in Memphis. He talked to the judge assigned to my case and promised I would seek rehabilitation and therapy. I was released on Elvis's recognizance with a year's probation.

After several days Elvis saw to it that I checked into the Tennessee Psychiatric and Drug Rehabilitation Hospital of Memphis. This was no Betty Ford Center. It was a state hospital, and it was rough. Amazed and horrified, I watched addicts scream in anguish and pain as they detoxed. I was feeling none too good, either. I stayed ten days, and then, to my regret, I left against medical advice. But I had received a real lesson in what drug abuse leads to, and I still had enough self-control left at that point to cut down on my intake through sheer will power.

The next time I was around Elvis, he acted like nothing had happened. He welcomed me back. I was on the road for only a short time when I came down with hepatitis. Again, I called Robyn for emotional support. She also took my calls when I went back out on the road.

During the last eighteen months of his life, Elvis became a physical and emotional wreck. I was supposed to be "taking care of him," but I wasn't doing much of a job taking care of me. I was one of the "lifers" who sat outside his door while he slept. Someone always kept an eye on him—around the clock. On more than one occasion I found him lying on the floor, or in bed, not breathing. His "sleeping medications" knocked him out so soundly, if only for short periods, that he could fall into positions that cut off his air. An overdose was inevitable for one of us, but we didn't think or talk about it.

I needed a "lifer" myself. I began doing drugs that no one else would take with me. I repulsed even myself. I had a monkey on my back that absorbed every penny I could lay my hands on.

In the middle of August 1977, we were scheduled for another tour: Portland, Maine; then Utica and Syracuse, New York; Hartford, Connecticut; Uniondale, New York; and on to Lexington, Kentucky; Roanoke, Virginia; Fayetteville, Tennessee; Asheville,

North Carolina; and finally back to Memphis for two shows at the Mid-South Coliseum.

Elvis was horribly depressed. The "bodyguard book," or *Elvis: What Happened?* by Red and Sonny West and Dave Hebler had just come out two weeks before. As in the case of Elvis's breakup with Priscilla, Elvis tried to avoid the substance of the issues the book presented by vilifying his opponents.

Red and Sonny West, as I've discussed, were for many years trusted members of the TCB crew—Red and Elvis's friendship went back to high school. Dave Hebler, a karate champion, had come on the payroll as security after meeting Elvis in 1972.

In the early 1970s, a number of serious death threats were made against Elvis's life. Once, FBI agents were stationed in his Vegas audience. The Tate-LaBianca murders by the Manson family in the 1960s and Patty Hearst's kidnapping in the '70s, made celebrities increasingly security conscious. Elvis felt more and more threatened and instructed his men to take a macho, aggressive attitude toward outsiders. Red, Sonny, Dave, and my brother, David, often had to use force to protect Elvis in public. Everyone toted guns—inspired by their employer who often gave firearms away as presents and had an impressive collection of his own.

Soon the scuffles of Elvis's security men with belligerent fans created problems. A serious lawsuit grew out of one fracas in Lake Tahoe, in which a man who had bribed his way, he thought, into a party took a serious beating after he turned off the lights in Elvis's hotel suite. Lisa Marie was with Elvis at the time, and the thought of a kidnapping pumped more adrenalin into everybody than the situation warranted. Sonny West, in particular, addressed the man's intrusion.

Elvis feared the financial problems such lawsuits created. He must also have grown disaffected with the older members of his crew for other reasons. They were middle-aged men, now, with families. They could not be at his beck and call in exactly the same ways as in the old days. Elvis increasingly liked family members around him. He liked my brothers and me, I'm sure, partly because our youth reminded him of how it had been, and we were ready to do anything and everything just for the chance of keeping our jobs, as the older guys no longer were.

Elvis decided to let Red, Sonny, and Dave go. Vernon fired them on July 13, 1976, saying the organization needed to cut down on the staff to save money. He gave them three-days' notice and one week's severance pay. Red and Sonny had devoted half a lifetime to working with Elvis; they deserved better than this. They had good reason to be angry.

Before the book's release, the three claimed they had written it as a warning to Elvis that he was destroying himself. I doubt the project started out that way. They were hotheads, and their first motive must have been to "get theirs." The book could actually have served this purpose, though, if Elvis had seen the disparity between his image and his personal life as something that needed to be reconciled. Instead, he raged against the three and caused scenes in which Jerry Schilling and Joe Esposito and the rest of us had to calm him down. Jerry and Joe were particularly good about reminding him that Lisa Marie would probably mind having a daddy with a drug problem less than having a daddy who was a murderer.

On Monday, August 15, a day before we were to leave on tour, I called Robyn. Her parents and she had moved to Destin, Florida. She had written a letter to me, expressing her concern for what she sensed I was going through.

When I got her on the phone I found out that she had been having nightmares about me in which she saw me dead and in hell. Her dreams, as I see it now, were translating the warning signals I was giving her into vivid images. I was about as dead as you can be as a person while still walking around. My life had grown hellish.

She told me that I needed to believe in Christ. She said he could take the drugs away and make me happy to be alive again. Once again, I said, "Not yet."

"What's it going to take?" she asked.

I didn't know, and I'm glad I didn't, since if I had I'm not sure I wouldn't have acted on the suicidal tendencies Robyn perceived in me.

After we got off the phone, Robyn and her mother got down on their knees and prayed for me. They asked the Lord two things specifically: "Please bring Rick to you, Lord, and remove him from the lifestyle that is proving so destructive." Her nightmares ended with that prayer.

Later, I went upstairs to check on Elvis and deliver his first round of sleeping medications. It was about 3 A.M., Tuesday, August 16—the hour before dawn when Elvis usually went to sleep. He was lying in the midst of piles of books on his big king-sized bed. One of the books was a Bible; the others related to the Shroud of Turin and spiritual issues.

I told Elvis about my conversation with Robyn. For seven years she had been talking to me about my need for Christ.

"She's right, Rick," he said. "You know that, don't you?"

I was shocked and stared at him uncomprehendingly. He looked so tired. So bewildered. He had his pajamas on with a silk robe. He hadn't yet had his sideburns colored for the tour, so they were a little long with a tinge of gray. I thought they looked great.

I remembered Elvis's talk with Rex Humbard in his hotel suite in Las Vegas. Contrary to his reported disdain toward ministers, in the years I toured with him, Elvis always sought out ministers; he was more ready to admit them backstage than anybody else—something I know at first hand since I handled such arrangements. Elvis huddled with Rex Humbard with a Bible open, studying the Scriptures, for several hours that day in Vegas, excluding all other visitors. A few years later, when I became concerned about Elvis's true beliefs, I talked with Rex Humbard about their conversation. He said that the questions Elvis asked and all his comments indicated that he understood quite well the Christian view of salvation. The foundation of his faith remained, despite the spiritualist overlays that came in the 1960s. That night Elvis confirmed to my satisfaction that those overlays were no longer there.

Elvis waved the pages of the bodyguard book at me. "What am I going to do about this, Rick?" he asked me.

I tried to make some reassuring comments about the fans not really caring. Why should anyone believe something written out of spite?

But Elvis saw things more clearly. "Let's pray," he said. He motioned me over to the side of the bed alongside of him. I was moved by this exhibition of his sincerity.

"Dear Lord," he prayed, "please show me a way. I'm tired and confused, and I need your help." (Unless you are going to demand a perfect act of contrition, that seems like a pretty decent sinner's prayer to me.) He looked up and said something to me that I shall remember until my dying day. "Rick," he said softly, "we should all begin to live for Christ."

I loved him. Not because he was the king of rock 'n' roll, or because he had a mansion, or for any other reason. I loved him because he was my big brother. He was a pitiful sight compared to the way I had seen him since I was five years old, but I loved him. I sat at the foot of his bed that night, and something inside me cried out for him. We were both hurting, but the real pressure was all his to bear. I wanted so desperately to help him. I remembered the time when several of the guys were jumping my case, and he shut them up by telling them to leave me alone—that I would have a big impact on the youth of this country some day. I thought he was joking, but he believed in me when few others did. He realized that I could communicate with people and that I was teachable. He had always bailed me out, yet I was helpless to do the same for him.

I left. Around 4 A.M., I delivered Elvis's second packet of sleeping medications. He got out of bed and went to the door of his bathroom. He turned and looked at me and said, "Rick, I won't need anything else for the rest of the night. If I do, I'll call and let you know." That meant not to disturb him for the rest of the night. He wanted either to sleep or to be alone with his girlfriend, Ginger Alden. She remained with him that night.

I told him good night at the doorway, quietly closed the door, and left.

I was strung out and tired from staying up all night myself, and I went down to the basement bedroom next to the bar and gameroom where so many Graceland parties took place, and downed several Demerol tablets. They knocked me out cold.

When Elvis called down about an hour later for his third medications packet, Aunt Delta Mae could not find me, and she took the packet up to him herself. Later, his private nurse delivered more sleeping medications. How many times I have regretted my own dependency. I can't escape the feeling that if I had been "straight" on the job, I may have saved Elvis from the consequences of the next few hours as I had many times before. No, my guilt feelings notwithstanding, Elvis's death was inevitable. If not then, later. The seeds of destruction had taken too deep a root.

Almost everyone who has written about Elvis has engaged in their own guilt-reducing exercises—it wasn't their fault, they all say in chorus. Well, I'm here to tell you, it was everybody's fault. John Lennon said, "It's the courtiers who kill the king." He was right. Each of us in Elvis's entourage bears his measure of responsibility for participating in such an insane life. I was too out of control and messed up to see that I was serving as an unwitting instrument in my stepbrother's destruction. It's not surprising, in a horrible way, that I was out of it just at the time when he took his last drug-induced ride into unconsciousness. I thought I was "taking care of him," but I couldn't take care of myself; about the only thing I really could have offered him in those days would have been a refusal to play the game. I should have stood up and said, "This is crazy!" But I was too intent on getting crazy myself. Caring enough to confront was not a part of my approach to relationships at that time in my life. Yes, Elvis died, not only because of his sins, but ours as well.

Elvis's last girlfriend, Ginger Alden, was asleep in Elvis's bedroom that morning. They had returned from a predawn session of racquetball with cousin Billy Smith and his wife, Jo. Ginger, a dark, doe-eyed, twenty-year-old, was asleep while Elvis went into the bedroom-sized dressing area of his bathroom to read. Ginger made him promise not to fall asleep. She was becoming aware of the risks he ran should the drugs hit and cause him to lose consciousness while alone.

David came on duty about twelve. He found me in the basement bedroom, groggy-eyed, but coming around by this time. I told him Elvis did not want to be disturbed until four o'clock. He understood what that meant. He had a friend there, and they decided to shoot some pool.

I left Graceland and met some friends at Grisanti's for lunch. Suddenly, as the waitress was bringing my order, I knew I had to get back to Graceland. Something was terribly wrong. Something had happened to Elvis. I had never had such a premonition before, and none since, but evidently the love and sympathy I had extended Elvis had established a spiritual bond between us with lines of communication that I can't fathom and wouldn't want to guess at.

Ginger woke up about two o'clock in the afternoon and discovered the bed empty beside her. She found Elvis lying face down in his dressing area, his knees curled up under him, his forehead touching the ground, his head twisted slightly to the right. When she looked at his face, she realized he was in trouble. Cold to the touch, she heard only a bit of trapped air escape his lungs when she tried to rouse him.

I came on the scene when the ambulance was pulling out. I got out of my car, my heart already pounding, and headed for the door. When I went through the back way and stepped into the kitchen, I felt a cold, weird sensation. It felt as if I had opened up a cold food locker and entered the twilight zone.

I walked through the house and noticed no one had touched the trunks packed for the tour. We were due at the airport soon. The men who were supposed to be moving the trunks just sat there. I remember throwing orders over my shoulder that they should get a move on. They stared at me as if I were from another country.

I walked into the kitchen and said, "What's going on? What are y'all doin'? Why isn't anybody working?"

One of the housekeepers looked up at me and asked, "You don't know, Ricky?"

"Know what?"

"Elvis is dead," she blurted out and started crying. "They found Elvis dead."

I felt nothing because I did not believe her. I had heard of people throwing up this kind of mental barrier and always considered it ridiculous. Yet, there I was, hearing the maid but not believing her for a moment.

I ran around the corner to Grandma's room, and when I cracked opened the door and saw Vernon and Dodger crying together there, Elvis's death hit me. I said to myself, "He's gone," as if only when I had heard it from myself would I believe it.

It was as if eternity had caved in. That's how it felt at the time. Like many of Elvis's fans, I had placed Elvis at the center of my world. I had made my life, as far as possible, an extension of his. About Elvis, Priscilla wrote, "Over the years, he became my father, husband, and very nearly God." My list would run brother, pal, father, and again, very nearly God. My denial of his death testified to how much my life was based on his. Now I experienced what Elvis did when Gladys died, the dilemma of how to go on when the person you have been living for—the person who has served as your idol, whom you love more than anyone else in the world—proves mortal.

In the next few minutes, I somehow managed to walk outside to the front steps. I had to get out of the house; all of the life had gone out of the mansion. It was cold . . . so cold. Stepping out the door I ran headlong into total chaos. Graceland was engulfed in confusion. Real people seemed to be acting out some kind of wild fictional story.

The phone started to ring and never stopped. People were going from room to room, not knowing what to do. There was talk of a press release; stupid things were causing all kinds of arguments. I couldn't cope with it. I couldn't think clearly.

For the first time in my life, my home became intolerable to me. I ran out the gates to a friend's house, past the gathering crowds. People who knew me tried to talk to me, but I couldn't stop, couldn't speak, couldn't face the truth. The media had already arrived. I avoided them as much as possible.

Robyn called. She had already heard. She had been trying to get through to me because she knew what kind of shape I would be in. In a matter of hours, every nation on the planet learned of Elvis's death. Not everyone knew my feelings, though, but Robyn did. Her friendship was the only thing of which I was certain at that time. She asked me if I wanted her to come. I did.

She flew in from Florida on the following day. I sat in the living room at Graceland, waiting for her arrival. Elvis's body lay in state in the center of the room, just below the chandelier. He was in a copper-lined coffin and wore a white suit and a pale blue shirt. As I sat there staring at him, trying to shut out the commotion around us, I will never forget how much he looked at peace. I watched him many nights when he would toss and turn in anguish. Now, there was no anguish in his face. He looked remarkably regal. Bright slashes of afternoon sunlight filled the foyer, reflected on the coffin, and rested on his face. He looked like the "king" he was.

Thousands of people were outside; hundreds more were in the house. Countless flowers formed a rainbow of color. I still looked at him, trying to understand the moment. But I couldn't. I couldn't understand anything. Usually when people lose a loved one, their attitude is either to run from God or to him. All I could think about was why God had allowed this to happen. Why?

I looked up in time to see Robyn trying to make her way through the people. When she reached my side, I noticed the small, white New Testament in her hand. I just stood up and held her. She knew that my grief was more than her words could match, so she said nothing. She simply held me. Robyn could see that I was bitter and confused, so she comforted me with presence and not preaching. This was a turning point in my life, and I would need her now more than I knew.

After a while, Robyn and I took a walk around Graceland, toward the back. We stood on a knoll that overlooked the mansion, the center of the Elvis Presley Empire. I saw that I could no longer escape the past. The past and the present were now one and the same, leaving me nowhere to go.

Elvis's fans lined up literally for miles to view his body. Vernon said that we owed it to them. But it was almost beyond endurance for the family and for many of the fans themselves.

Ambulances raced through the Memphis heat to revive people who had been stricken by the combination of the sun and their sorrow. They were young and old, rich and poor. They came from everywhere to pay a final tribute to Elvis. There were enough tears shed on the grounds that day to supply a river. I saw and felt their shock and disbelief, which served to magnify my own feelings. I wanted to comfort them and be comforted by them, but I couldn't reach out to them. I was helpless.

I moved through the final scenes as if it were all a dream. Their faces, however, kept jolting me back to the reality that Elvis was truly gone. He had given much to the world, much more than he knew. I knew that he would be remembered for his music, but I also knew that he should be remembered for his humanitarianism. He really cared for others. Many of his generous acts were done secretly, never seeking the praise of others. He donated huge sums to the underprivileged, to police funds, and to orphanages.

Elvis's touch on my life was similar, in a way, to the millions of fans who never knew him. It has to do with a sense of gratitude, love, and memories. I found a sense of inspiration from him. He offered a link to people and the fulfillment of their dreams. When they lost him, they lost some of their dreams. Of course, I know now that the only way to be free from the pain of emptiness is to be touched by the Lord. But I didn't know that then. I could truly identify with Elvis's fans the world over. I knew that they felt the loss as surely as I was feeling it. And I wasn't handling it well at all.

August 19, 1977 is carved into my memory as if time has stood still. It was then that I said good-bye to Elvis forever. The funeral was very difficult for me. All the flowers and condolences from around the world didn't make a dent in my grief. The service was held at the house as gospel music filled the air. Rex Humbard and C. W. Bradley officiated. It was not a positive service by any standard. Lisa Marie was nine years old, so sweet, so sad. Priscilla sat beside her. Some celebrities, close friends, and the family were all that were present.

Internment took place following the service. While we were moving the coffin to the hearse, one of the huge limbs from the tree overhanging the house split and came crashing down directly in front of the lead car. Everything stopped until the limb could be removed. It was a strange thing. The day was sunny, and there was almost no wind. Some people were chilled by the unusual timing of the thing. I heard someone say, "Well, he's still with us, making sure that we do it up right." It took several policemen to move the fallen limb from the drive; the delay was unsettling for many of us.

Finally the hearse moved on from Graceland to Forest Hills Cemetery. Sixteen white limousines formed the stately entourage. Thousands of people lined the streets on each side of the ten-mile stretch. The Memphis Police Department turned out in full dress uniform. Helicopters flew overhead, and people held their kids on their shoulders in silent respect.

As we drove to the cemetery, that sea of faces etched itself on my mind. Few people had this kind of effect on so many others. Everyone knew that Elvis wasn't perfect, but they loved him for his music and for who he was. I loved him for the love he had given me.

After Elvis's coffin was placed next to his mother's in the giant white mausoleum, we spent a brief time there and then finally returned to Graceland. Then everybody left. People I had grown up with, loved, and lived with were now suddenly gone.

Emptiness overwhelmed me. Unanswered questions angered and haunted me. I had nowhere to go, no sense of direction. The road I had been following was gone. I was alone.

Some people have speculated about whether Elvis committed suicide. They have pointed out that he did not eat his usual meals that final day, and he may have saved up his medication packets. They say that in his loneliness and desperation, he finally made one last extreme gesture and took the drugs all at once. The fact is, we will never know for certain. The coroner's statement said that Elvis died of heart failure. The lab report showed the presence of fourteen drugs in Elvis's system, some of them at greater-than-toxic levels, and suggested strongly that Elvis died of polypharmacy, or the mortal interaction of a combination of drugs. That's all we know as far as the hard facts are concerned. A wide variety of speculations can be made by just about anyone with as little evidence as that. As for me, I don't believe and never have believed that Elvis deliberately, consciously committed suicide. He would never have done that to Lisa Marie, especially while she was at Graceland. He loved her too much.

Elvis said that an image is a hard thing to live up to. It seemed, in his final years, his image became too much of a burden to live with. He clowned on stage, played to the band, often tried to show up his own act as a joke. But the fans stayed hooked, and Elvis stayed hooked, too. Only his death let him off. The rumor exists that Elvis faked his death to slip away from the fans and their demands. He would never have done this. Again, he cared too much about Lisa Marie. Besides, twenty thousand people viewed his body. Several witnesses were at the autopsy. How much proof do you need? No, Elvis was dead, and I felt that a part of me had died as well.

# 11

## Burning Love

After the funeral, I stayed in Memphis for a while. I did not know what to do with myself, other than get high. I soon found out that Elvis had left his entire inheritance to Lisa Marie, with Vernon as executor, and after his passing, Priscilla. Even at the time I was grateful for empty pockets, since I might well have followed Elvis into the grave via narcotics. He had done more than enough for me in his lifetime, and I was grateful.

I knew I needed a new life. I sold the Triumph TR6 that Elvis had given me and went out to California. Everyone who had worked for Elvis had connections in the entertainment industry. I called up some people I knew and pursued a job for an independent television crew.

I tried to sober up, but when my job put some money in my pockets, I quickly joined the Hollywood party scene. Addictions to alcohol and other drugs are progressive. When you stop and start again you don't go back to the beginning. You start right where you left off, or even beyond that. So I was well on the way to destroying myself in no time.

I was staying with some friends. One night I came into the kitchen, cranked on cocaine and Quaaludes. Standing at the counter, I felt my legs go weak. The next thing I knew I was on the floor. I rolled around a bit and laughed to cover my embarrassment. I looked up to see if my hosts were enjoying the joke.

They glared at me in a way that made me stand right back up. My friend's wife fixed me with her eyes. "Ricky," she said, "you are going to die. Do you want that? You want to crawl in beside your brother in his coffin?"

To me she had said enough, but she hadn't finished. "You are going to die, and no one is going to mourn for you like they did for Elvis. You are just another punk junky without enough money to be put in the ground properly. Wake up! No one even wants to mess with you any more. This isn't cool. This is death. You are going out. No one's there to rescue you. The person I knew as Ricky is dead already and we're just left with his needle tracks. I wish I cared more than I do. Part of me thinks it will be a relief to have you dead."

I think she shocked herself with that last statement, and when she heard the last echoes of her tirade bounce back to her and seemed to recognize that she meant every word, she stalked off and left me to myself.

I knew what she said was true, and I did not want to die. I needed help and wasn't sure I still had the kind of friends who could supply anything more than the next fix.

I called Robyn. She heard the desperation in my voice and invited me to visit her family in Florida. I was on the next plane.

I arrived in Destin, Florida on a Wednesday. My hair had grown down to my waist, I had nothing but t-shirts, jeans, and flip-flops to wear, and, at an even six feet, I weighed about 120 pounds.

Robyn was shocked at my appearance. Still, she welcomed me and tried to cover her concern. She listened to me talk on the way in from the airport. She did not get on my case when I asked that we stop at a store so I could buy a beer. I was so nervous my knees were hopping in that car.

Robyn talked to me about her faith. I was polite and non-committal. She asked me to go to church that next night. No way, I said. She said I had tried everything else but Jesus, what did I have to lose? I could wear my t-shirt and jeans. That surprised me, but I kept saying no.

When we arrived at the door, and I saw the impression I made on her mother, I was grateful she actually let me in.

The next day, when I woke up, Robyn had already left the house. Her mother told me she had gone to see her pastor, to pray for me. I felt very uncomfortable talking to her mom and contemplated leaving.

Later that day, as Robyn and I walked on the beach, I listened to her talk about her faith. I began to realize how much Robyn, her family, friends, and people I didn't even know, like her pastor, were concerned about me. These people had been having long talks about Ricky Stanley and praying for him. It hadn't done me much good, I thought, but I appreciated their concern. I decided to go to church with Robyn that night.

Robyn attended one of the Jesus Movement churches that sprang up in the 1970s. Dressing like I did was normal there—in fact, if you didn't dress like I did you looked out of place. I noticed, though, that the other latter-day hippies looked a lot more together than me. They sat in couples, sometimes with their children around them, and they looked happy without seeming smug or sanctimonious. This was church all right, but without so much of the false piety that I remembered from the past.

Then Jay Zinn, the preacher, rose to speak. I knew that he had been a surfer, and that helped break down my resistance. He began to speak from Matthew 7 about our not judging others. I looked around. No one was looking at me. I relaxed. He said that only God can judge, because only he looks on the heart. Only he knows us truly, beyond what even we know of ourselves.

This impressed me. I had been raised in a judgmental kind of Christianity, and most Christians I met who heard I was associated with Elvis Presley promptly had me boxed up and ready to ship off to hell. After everything I had been through, I knew it would take a God to make a proper reckoning.

His words continued as he quoted from the Scriptures: "'Enter in at the narrow gate; for wide is the gate, and broad is the way, that leadeth to destruction, and many there be who go that way.'"

I had chosen the broad path. That was all too clear. What could there be for me in this?

"'Beware of false prophets,'" Jay Zinn continued, "'who come to you in sheep's clothing, but inwardly they are ravenous wolves.'"

He continued reading, "because narrow is the gate, and hard is the way, which leads unto life, and few there be that find it."

Somewhere in the service I began to take these Scriptures personally. I had no hope of finding the narrow gate any more. I saw my mother's face when she saw me after my arrest. The look of disappointment on Vernon's. I remembered Robyn's pleading countenance when she talked to me after my first drug rehab. The wild, abandoned horror of the faces of my fellow addicts at the hospital as they stared at my face as if in a mirror. The look on Elvis's face when those elevator doors opened after my arrest and he stood there, waiting, loving me even in disappointment. For the first time I began to feel God at work in my heart.

When the preacher finished speaking, he asked for those who wanted to accept Christ to raise their hands. Mine shot up almost without my thinking about it. Robyn looked at me, amazed.

I was the only one who raised a hand that night, and I was invited to talk with the preacher afterward.

In his office, Jay asked me, "What's the deal, Rick?"

"What do you mean, 'what's the deal'?" I replied. "What's your deal? You asked me if I wanted to know more about God or Jesus or the Lord or something, and I'm here to find out. I'm wondering really if he will have anything to do with me."

He looked at me and smiled. "He sure will!"

His quick confidence made me skeptical. Did this guy know what I had been through? The things I had done! I felt like I had laid down a mile or so of that broad path all by myself.

I leaned forward and looked at him closely. A nearby light cast a shadow over one side of his face, highlighting and opening up, it seemed, his right eye. His hands were clasped in a way that conveyed an unearthly yet gentle strength. As we talked he impressed me as a straightforward and down-to-earth guy; he was talking about things he believed in, but I didn't feel he was trying to sell me on anything. He recognized that my choices were mine, and that my relationship with God depended on his actions toward me. If God didn't make himself real to me, there wasn't a whole lot Jay could do about it. He could only tell me that God had made himself real to him.

Finally, I said, "Look, friend. I want to know the whole ball of wax. I want to know what this deal is all about."

He tilted his head slightly, and the shadow left his face. He stared at me, both eyes penetrating. "You know you are a sinner, don't you?"

I had no trouble determining that.

"You know that Christ died for you?"

"I believe that, too," I said. "I don't know why he did, but I believe it."

"I don't know either," he said, almost whispering. He asked me whether I wanted to pray with him.

I did. I had things I wanted to say to God now, if he were really there to hear me. We began to pray. I asked, with sincerity and caution and some doubt, for Jesus to be real to me. For him to forgive me. For him to renew my life."

Suddenly, unexpectedly, and to me, miraculously, it happened! In an instant, the Spirit of God came upon me in a way that was overwhelming. I felt waves of warm, pure love that overflowed and filled my spirit and body. I felt this love burn through me, searing away everything of which I was ashamed, leaving me as if newborn. A miracle of astounding proportions took place in my life. God knew it would take a strong dose of his love and his power to make me his, and he gave me just what I needed. The incredible sense of forgiveness was beyond description. It was like a weight was lifted from me. Lights seemed to burn brighter. Sounds were clearer.

Later, when I met Robyn at the car, I realized that I no longer had any desire to do drugs. Or even smoke cigarettes. These addictions had been lifted from me.

God, through Jesus Christ, his son, comes to people in many ways; sometimes, as in the apostle Paul's case, or mine, he comes dramatically. Sometimes, as in the biblical Timothy's case or

Robyn's, he comes through the nurturing love of a good family. Those of us who are furthest away when he crosses the distance and makes us his own often have a vivid awareness of his *action* in this process; it's as if we catch the momentum of his approach. However the Lord comes, he brings with him his love, his burning, cleansing love, and his peace.

My encounter with Jesus Christ put me on that narrow path. I've never wanted to waver from it. The Lord's grace has steadied me and kept me walking.

I lived with Jay Zinn for a while, which offered me intense discipling, guidance, and accountability. He taught me the disciplines of praying, Scripture reading, and studying. Then I received my first invitation to speak about my former life with Elvis and my new life with the Lord. I was to speak in Pearl, Mississippi, but first I had to fly into Jackson.

I was in for one of the biggest jolts of my life when the plane landed. I couldn't believe what I saw. There were two hundred teenagers at the airport to greet me. They had posters that said, "He served the king of rock 'n' roll . . . Now he serves the King of kings." I'll never forget that greeting for as long as I live. It was fantastic, and it was a little weird. This was so strange to me. For years I had seen crowds and banners and shouted greetings for Elvis. But this was directed toward me—and for a completely different reason. In a flash, I had a message. These people wanted to hear that message. And I realized at that moment why I went through all that I had as a child and a teenager. Why was I Elvis's brother? Why was I a Christian? I was to take all of the glory that surrounded the king of rock 'n' roll and point it to the King of kings.

On that summer night—July 3, 1978—I went to the podium in front of thousands of people. The crowd hushed. This was one of the most emotional moments in my life. I looked out across thousands of faces, glanced at the evening sky above, and silently prayed, "Dear God, give me some words to say."

I opened my mouth suddenly and said, "The last time I was here was with my brother. This time, I am here representing a new king—Jesus Christ." The people went wild. They cheered and jumped out of their seats. The overwhelming power of God's love was like bolt of lightning.

I only spoke for about ten or twelve minutes, but in that time God confirmed my vocation as an evangelist.

In this confirmation, God did not offer me, as Colonel Parker did later, my own kingdom, fame, or power. The Lord did not offer anything that I could control or even mistake for "mine." He offered only to be there for me, and to speak through me. He offered a relationship. This relationship is characterized by a love that respects who I am as a person, that nurtures my gifts and that calls me to become someone who dares to grow beyond the limits of his own imagination. To be a servant.

God's love is tough, too. It chastens me when I get out of line; it's not the love of the courtiers for the king, it's the love of a wise parent for his children. The Lord offered to love me unconditionally, and to forgive my every failure, but to excuse nothing.

God offered me what Elvis so desperately needed—love. We are all caught in that trap, our need for love, our need to find ourselves in relationships with others. For we cannot know ourselves, we cannot be ourselves, alone. One of the mysteries of being human is that we are so divided within ourselves, so at a loss in ourselves, that we search desperately for someone within whose eyes we can see ourselves aright. That's why so many of us live out our lives trying to please others. Elvis had Gladys; I had Elvis. As Bob Dylan wrote, "You gotta serve somebody."

Or at least, some thing. That's also why so many people become materialistic or tote up the number of their various kinds of conquests. They don't know who they are, and they think that if they can say, "I'm the guy making a hundred thousand a year," or "I'm the woman who dated Elvis Presley," then their constant doubts will be cured.

Living for yourself is meaningless. In your heart of hearts, you know you are no one, or not much good, or both. If you take money, or sex, or drugs, or Elvis, or yourself, though, as your god, it doesn't work either. We are all born with a God-shaped void within our souls that only God can fill.

I know that people who believe this often live lives indistinguishable from people who don't. At one level, Elvis believed this. In practice, unfortunately, he made his image his god. He knew the truth, but he served a false god, and that destroyed him.

Surely the God of the universe will do right, and I leave Elvis, who prayed for God to show him the way, in his hands. It's not up to us to judge him, but we can certainly learn from his life. No one is made to handle the kind of love and adoration Elvis received. An image is not only a hard thing to live up to, it's a killer.

Straight is the gate and narrow the way. A hard saying, but what does it profit a man, if he gains the whole world, and loses his own soul? My yoke is easy, and my burden light, says the Lord. Take it from a young man who was once virtually dead, and is now, thank God, alive.

Good-bye, my brother. I will see you again. We are all living for Jesus now.

# Questions and Answers

The following section addresses the many questions that I have been asked over the years about Elvis. They are arranged topically.

## Style, Talent, and Musical Taste

**Q: Where did Elvis learn his style?**

A: It evolved over the years, but between his eleventh and thirteenth years, Elvis regularly visited radio station WELO in Tupelo to watch performers live. Undoubtedly he picked up some things there as well as from the all-night gospel sings he attended, but in reality, Elvis's style was unique to him. During his high school years in Memphis, he listened a lot to the local black R&B station WDIA. No doubt that had its influence. But when Elvis first burst on the scene in the mid fifties, nobody had seen anything like him before.

**Q: What specifically caused Elvis when he was sixteen to change his hairstyle and clothes into what later became his trademark?**

A: He saw a movie starring Tony Curtis called *City Across the River.* He identified with the main character's situation (not unlike his own economic background) and hairstyle. Elvis's condition and temperament were well suited to being influenced by this story.

**Q: How was Elvis able to withstand the mocking and jeering of his peers?**

A: Red West for some reason felt sorry for Elvis and became his "protector." Red was feared by his peers and later became one of the "Memphis Mafia." Also, the opinion of his peers never really meant that much to him. Because of this, he became a strong individual.

**Q: Do you attach a great deal of significance to this change of style to Elvis's overall personality development?**

A: Yes. It was almost like a second birth for Elvis. As he gradually began to identify more and more with the tough image he tried to portray, he actually became that way.

**Q: Would you agree with some writers of Elvis biographies that Elvis's sixteenth year was his most decisive?**

A: Yes, he changed hair and clothes style and joined the ROTC and won his school's annual variety show. It was the year the shy, poor boy "made good" and finally felt accepted. It was an inordinately influential year. All this while going through the final changes of puberty. Elvis's sixteenth year must have imprinted some substantial marks on his personality. In fact, in many ways Elvis never did outgrow his sixteenth year. He was like a sixteen-year-old in many ways the rest of his life. This was one of the most significant traps Elvis ever got caught in. Like his overnight success, the "trauma" of his sixteenth year came fast with little preparation educationally or emotionally to enable Elvis to process it maturely. In fact, change was very hard for him in all areas of his life.

**Q: Is it true that early in Elvis's career he identified with Rudolph Valentino?**

A: Yes. Tommy Neal, an early friend of Elvis, remembers a conversation with Elvis about this. Basically it didn't take Elvis long to realize that the essence of his ability to move an audience was "sex appeal," and he spent considerable time cultivating this image so that by the time RCA signed him on November 21, 1955, that image was almost complete.

**Q:** There has been much speculation about who was really responsible for giving Elvis his first big break. Did Elvis ever comment on that?

**A:** Yes. He had no doubt that it was Marion Keisker. Marion ran the recording service for Sam Phillips and was the first to meet Elvis when he came in to record a song for a birthday present for Gladys. Elvis often said that it was Marion who mentioned him to Sam Phillips several times until a song came in that Marion convinced Sam to let Elvis record. The song proved too difficult for Elvis, but during the sessions he improved. Eventually Elvis recorded "That's All Right," which launched his career.

**Q:** Concerning Elvis's style, it has been said that his greatest genius was his marvelous ability to mimic. True?

**A:** To a point. True, Elvis combined his ability to mimic gospel, country, and R&B into a new form called "rock-a-billy" or later "rock and roll." But it takes a real talent to blend old styles into something new. Actually, there was no one to imitate when it came to singing rock 'n' roll. As John Lennon said, "Before Elvis, there was nothing." Combining styles, yes; mimicking, no. Unfortunately in his later years this genius became a trap as he found it difficult to change his style. Of course his fans demanded the "old Elvis" and so the trap simply came full circle.

**Q:** Did Elvis ever write any of his own songs?

**A:** No. His genius was in interpreting other people's songs in a way that made them uniquely his. When he sang a song that had been recorded by someone else, you forgot about the first version and were really convinced you were hearing it for the first time. He had an extraordinary ability to emote and transfer his music to fit his style and image.

**Q: What are some especially memorable songs that Elvis reinvented?**

A: James Taylor's "Steamroller," Simon and Garfunkel's "Bridge over Troubled Water," Creedence Clearwater Revival's classic "Proud Mary," and Marty Robbins's "You Gave Me a Mountain" are four good examples. Of course Mickey Newberry's "American Trilogy" is his best known, combining "Dixie," "All My Trials," and "The Battle Hymn of the Republic."

**Q: What was Elvis's personal taste in music?**

A: Mostly Elvis listened to gospel music. Wherever he went he carried a case of a hundred or so albums, most of them gospel. It was his way of praising the Lord and about the closest Elvis came to worshiping God in the traditional sense. Mahalia Jackson was his favorite gospel singer. He wore her records out.

**Q: What kind of musician was Elvis? I know he played the guitar and piano. Was he very good?**

A: Compared to a professional, no, Elvis was never that good. But he was much better than average. Remember, he never had lessons, but he had some level of proficiency for drum, bass guitar, piano, and regular guitar. He even had an organ he tinkered with every now and then. He was a much better pianist than guitar player.

**Q: What was Elvis's philosophy of entertainment?**

A: He simply wanted people to enjoy the music he enjoyed. When they did, he felt he had accomplished something. Of course, he (like most entertainers) thrived on the high his fans gave him during a live performance. But Elvis really let his fans know that they were loved and appreciated. His famous "Thank you, thank you, very much," was not just a canned expression he used after each song. Even though many people have mimicked or made fun of this phrase, for Elvis, it was heartfelt and sincere. The adulation of his fans was always an humbling experience for him.

**Q: Several writers have said that while Elvis may have complained to his friends and family about his frustration at being handed roles only in mediocre films, in reality he had long since resigned himself to being a "property." Is that true?**

A: Partially true. Elvis was very naive when it came to business. He trusted Colonel Parker. Elvis also knew that he was making a lot of money. My guess is that if an opportunity to do something "risky" had come along and the Colonel had said, "Well, I don't think it's best for your image. You might destroy your career and alienate your fans, but if you want to, go ahead," Elvis would not have had the courage to do it. This doesn't mean that he didn't want new challenges. But nothing could outdo what he'd already accomplished musically. The only possible way to accomplish more would be through acting, and on this count he was clearly caught in a trap with the Colonel in control.

**Q: Is it true, as some have written, that allowing Colonel Parker to take complete control of his career was in the end ruinous to Elvis as an artist?**

A: The Colonel never told Elvis what songs to sing or how to read his lines in the movies. But locking Elvis into his publishers confined him to the kind of music they could obtain, thereby discouraging him from reaching out for better music. And by working out the formula for Elvis's movies and confining him to such pictures, the Colonel indirectly exercised considerable control over Elvis the artist. Whether Elvis's fans would have tolerated a change in the formula or whether Elvis could have ever become a great actor is another question.

## Image, Fame, and Fans

**Q: Was Elvis's image (the phenomenon generated by the early 1956 hits and television and radio appearances), in the long run, one of the greatest "traps" sprung on Elvis?**

A: Yes. His rise to superstardom was so meteoric that no one ever wanted to tinker with it. Musically, songs were crafted to fit his image, not challenge it. Movies packaged the image. The audience created in 1956–57 was so huge it really took until 1968 to saturate it with enough movies and movie tunes. The Elvis image had been imprinted on the minds of millions of impressionable teens, and the movie and music industries fed off this phenomenon for twelve years. "Don't mess with success," or better yet the phrase "dance with the one who brung ya," was never more true than it was regarding Colonel Parker's management of Elvis. Yet Elvis himself clearly became the victim of his popularity. If he liked a demo record presented to him, he felt that all he had to do was copy it and add his own idiosyncratic touches and it would be a hit. Of course, it was. Such was the nature of his enormous popularity, but it contributed to his decline as a creative force in music. Later he felt that he could no longer do what he had done in the '50s, and he was concerned that his audiences may not take to his love songs and ballads. Ironically, one proof of the public's preference for Elvis's early work can be seen in the overwhelming response generated by the U.S. Postal Service's poll regarding the 1993 Elvis stamp in favor of his younger image.

**Q: What would you say was the one most important reason for Elvis's explosive rise to fame?**

A: The youth culture of the fifties. It was history's first real culturally autonomous generation, the post-World War II baby boomers—a generation fed by movies, the new medium of

television, and radio. It was simply timing, like most successes in life—being at the right place at the right time—in
this case, with the greatest motivator and influence on teens:
music. Rock 'n' roll's condemnation by the adult world simply ensured its, and ultimately Elvis's, success. Also, Elvis
was very gifted musically, especially his voice, which even in
the last years, never deserted him. His gifts alone would have
made him a success, but not a phenomenon.

**Q: How much, really, was Elvis a prisoner of his fame?**

A: It was real trap. He couldn't go anywhere without being
mobbed. But even if Elvis exaggerated the problem, he believed it was true and behaved as if it were true. He allowed
either the reality or his belief to make him into a recluse in
his later years. But with the trap set, he knew that if people
didn't make a big deal in public, his career would be in
trouble.

**Q: When Elvis the image was finally "created," how did it
affect Elvis's personal life?**

A: Elvis became the image as much as was humanly possible.
The show never stopped. In style, substance, identity, and
behavior, he tried to live his own myth. He became "locked
in," a phrase I heard Elvis use several times. "Caught" is a
better word.

**Q: Did Elvis always want people around him because he
felt confined by his popularity?**

A: Yes. He couldn't just go out to a movie or restaurant and do
simple things like that. He made it confining for the rest of
us too. He wanted us around all the time. Generally, we really did want to be around him, but it was not something
negative. There were thousands of people who would have
gladly traded places with us.

**Q:** **Throughout his life, it's been said that Elvis knew that the "patronizing elite" of the highbrow establishment viewed him and his entourage as rubes, hillbillies, and hicks, but that they tolerated him for what he could produce for them. Is this true and, if so, how did Elvis handle it?**

**A:** I think he did suspect it. He commented often about the emptiness he found in Hollywood and Las Vegas, their pretentiousness and hypocrisy. He dealt with it by retreating into isolation, first with his friends and family and finally, almost totally alone within himself.

**Q:** **Is it true that Elvis had (and has) the most loyal fans in the history of entertainment?**

**A:** Unquestionably. They stayed with him through his army years, through years of mediocre movies, and the final years of less-than-perfect performances. But Elvis paid a price. His fans did not mind his taking on the trappings of success (pampered, expensively clad, luxuriously transported, extravagantly indulged) as long as he maintained exactly the same world-view or mentality that the fans originally shared. In effect, he could not grow as a human being, never make explicit criticisms. He could only remain passive and avoid controversy. He was always one of them—the fans. Elvis's fans caged him much more effectively than the record companies, movie producers, or songwriters. His own needs and desires were beside the point. Unfortunately, Elvis did not have the character and strength to fight it. I think he instinctively knew he'd risk losing it all if he changed. That prospect was just too scary to him. It takes a lot of courage to risk everything for creative and personal fulfillment. Most people, not just Elvis, would have failed that test. There is security in the familiar, and security was what his poverty-filled upbringing had taught him was the most important thing in life. Nevertheless, I'm sure he would be awed—and honored—by his continued popularity. Elvis may be more revered by his fans now than ever before. He's become a cultural folk hero.

**Q: Over the past fifteen years, you've talked with scores of people about your relationship with Elvis. You've heard thousands of fans express their love and appreciation of him. Is there a dominant theme in what these people say about Elvis?**

A: Yes. Most of them express to me how much his gospel music means to them. True, you would probably expect that since I mainly speak in church or religious settings, but the most often repeated comment is, "You'll never know the impact your brother's gospel songs have had upon my life."

## Work Habits, Working for Elvis, and Touring

**Q: How did Elvis manage to pull himself through three films per year and at least that many albums?**

A: Elvis, when he worked or played, was an extremely intense man. When he set his mind to a task, by sheer tenacity, he could push himself through. His high work ethic prevailed. He learned from the example of his mom and dad that you didn't have to love, or even like, your job. You just did it and you better be grateful you even had one. The fear of losing that job was always in Elvis's mind.

**Q: Is it true that Elvis's high work ethic kept him making mediocre films?**

A: Partially. He did view movies, like his music, as a job. Having been dirt poor he was realizing most of his youthful ambitions by simply having a steady job and making money. If his job gave him what he wanted, he was happy. And even if it robbed him of some of his self-respect, he would never refuse to work. You just didn't quit a good job. Unfortunately, this attitude and his respect for authority played right into the hands of the Hollywood establishment. They were only too glad to have a "cooperative" star, one whom they could manipulate. Elvis was defenseless against such power and sophistication. Also Hollywood was a different scene then. The studios controlled the actors. Stars today have a lot more power over what they do and who they work with.

**Q: I've read that working for Elvis didn't really pay much and that there was no real financial security for the future. Was that true?**

A:   Partially. We had medical insurance, and Elvis was very generous. It was fine for the single guys, but the "benefits" were in terms of immediate lifestyle, rather than long-term insurance or pensions. We lived just like Elvis (talk about fringe benefits!). On our own, none of us could have been able to afford to do that. Once some of the guys became husbands and fathers, however, it was more difficult. They still made a good salary, but in terms of the stress, hours, and talent needed for their jobs, they were probably underpaid compared to working for a corporation.

**Q: Where did the term "Memphis Mafia" come from?**

A:   After the filming of *G.I. Blues* in 1960, Elvis went through a short period where he insisted that all of the boys look professional and wear dark suits with white shirts and ties. One morning they all showed up in Las Vegas wearing sunglasses like a squad of hit men. The press dubbed them the "Memphis Mafia," and the name stuck.

**Q: Could the people who worked for Elvis be described as yes-men?**

A:   Everyone subordinated his identity to Elvis. Elvis's will was law, and he had difficulty tolerating things if they didn't go his way. We were all scared of Elvis's temper and did anything to avoid doing something that would set him off. In one way, Elvis really didn't have any true friends, if by that you mean someone from whom he would take advice. He was a very lonely man in that regard. True friends confront and risk being rejected. Not many people have friends like that.

**Q: What was life on the road like with Elvis?**

A: For newcomers, at first it was fun. Everything was exciting. But eventually one engagement led to another, and cities, faces, places, and parties passed into a ceaseless swirling blur of hard work, hijinks, dope, booze, and women. The glamour faded fast. You really can get too much of something. The selfish, hedonistic lifestyle is empty in the end. Nothing is special or unique anymore. So you do anything to escape the disillusionment of an is-this-all-there-is way of life.

**Q: I've heard that Elvis got really bored with Vegas and touring. Is that true?**

A: I'm sure that there were times when Elvis got tired of the same routine, especially when he was in physical pain, but to describe all of the last two years of his life as boring would be a mistake. In fact, in some ways you could say that his only source of happiness then was his fans. The concerts seemed to invigorate him.

**Q: What did touring really mean to Elvis?**

A: It was his life's blood. On stage he was in total control. He knew exactly what made people happy. He was in heaven. The performance was his identity—who he was. That's how he'd want to be remembered—as the greatest performer of all time, and I believe he was, especially in his prime. His relationship with his fans meant everything.

**Q: Why didn't Elvis ever play in foreign countries? Wasn't he as popular abroad as he was in the United States?**

A: Yes, and in some countries even more popular. He was once offered a million dollars for a single performance in England. No really good answer has ever been given for his not going abroad. Some people have said that Colonel Parker was not an American citizen and had a personal fear of crossing an American border and then not being able to return. That may be true. Elvis was planning a foreign tour for 1978, and had he lived he most likely would have made the tour—with or without the Colonel.

## Money, Generosity, and Hobbies

**Q: A lot has been said and written about Elvis's concept of money. How can it be described?**

A: He didn't value money. Only people who are extremely wealthy can understand. Those without money, who never seem to have enough, believe that more of it will solve all of their problems. If you really have all you need of anything, you tend to take it for granted, devalue it, almost hold it in contempt for not delivering the true happiness that you thought it promised when you didn't have it. All the gifts, the charity giving, the "throwing away" money was Elvis's way of saying, "Take it, it's only money, and there's always plenty more where that came from." Elvis commented more than once that the Bible says that what you give you get back tenfold. While he misunderstood the real meaning of that thought, he believed in this promise. People really are happiest when they are giving themselves away. Elvis was happiest when he was giving people stuff. True, he was compulsive and lacked maturity sometimes when he did extreme things, but it was his money and, compared to what most extremely wealthy people do with their money, Elvis comes off looking pretty good in this regard.

**Q:** **How could Elvis justify the kind of spending he did at age forty, so that he was almost broke, even though he had earned more than $100 million (three to four times that in today's money)?**

**A:** Elvis always believed money was there to spend. His parents never had any "extra" money, so he didn't have a role model. He also believed that he could always earn more by just touring, and he was right. His wildly extravagant spending sprees are exaggerated, although he did everything in excess. An example is that when Elvis finally got over his fear of flying, he soon owned a fleet of four multiengined aircraft when one airplane would have been sufficient. He often responded to Vernon's concern with, "Aw Daddy, it's just money." Unfortunately, as Elvis got older his reckless spending grew to insane proportions. In order to cover the debt, Elvis in 1974 had to play a staggering total of 152 shows, mostly one-night stands. The physical and emotional toll on him was enormous. In short, Elvis was never able to limit himself in any area of his life. He was always a little boy at heart in his thinking. He was accountable to no one but himself.

**Q:** **Why do you think Elvis was so generous with his money, automatically buying and giving away very expensive gifts, even at times to perfect strangers?**

**A:** There is no simple answer. There were many factors. From an early age Elvis was always generous. At nine, following the "baptism of the Holy Spirit" (a Pentecostal religious experience) he gave away a new tricycle. His early poverty could be a factor. He identified with those who had less than he did. Perhaps it was another attempt at getting the love he so desired. At times he probably did it as a way of saying "I'm sorry" to those he had wronged in some way. He loved to see people's expressions and response when the gift was given. Maybe he did it sometimes to get rid of guilt. The simplest answer is probably the best: It just made him happy. Some people say it was irresponsibility, but it gave him great joy, and being the compulsive person he was, he just did it often enough for it to seem odd.

**Q: Is it true that never once in the twenty-two years of his professional relationship with Colonel Parker did Elvis ever question the Colonel's business practices and how he handled Elvis's money?**

A: Yes. Elvis took everything on trust. He demanded absolute loyalty from those who worked for him directly, and even though in theory the Colonel was one of those employees, in practice it was actually the reverse. It was more like Elvis worked for the Colonel. Only after Elvis's death did the truth about the Colonel's management begin to come to the surface. It was never proved that the Colonel did anything illegal, but when you write the contracts and subsequently interpret their application, well, the temptation to make decisions in your favor is very real. The probate court dissolved the Colonel's relationship with the estate, which speaks volumes.

**Q: How do you explain Elvis's fascination with guns?**

A: He was a typical gun collector. He collected World War I and II rifles and handguns, and he received guns from many celebrities like Spiro Agnew and Paul Newman. Elvis enjoyed going to shooting ranges around Memphis. He was especially proud of the marksmanship medals he earned while in the army. He also shot skeet at his ranch. Not being a hunter, Elvis took target practice as a hobby. It wasn't an obsession; it was simply a hobby.

**Q: Why was Elvis so fascinated with collecting badges— police, deputy sheriffs, even a federal narcotics badge?**

A: He didn't just collect them, they were given to him by the proper authorities with authorization to use them. He even received the federal narcotics badge from President Nixon himself. As to why, well, those badges were potent symbols of authority and power. Elvis actually used them on numerous occasions. When he was just out of high school he wanted to be a highway patrolman. I think it was a power thing with Elvis, a way of controlling others. He was really a law-and-order nut. It was also fun for him. Imagine his stopping a car for speeding, flashing one of his badges for identification, and admonishing the startled driver to slow down. He got a real kick out of observing people's reactions.

**Q: Why do you think Elvis was so fascinated with cars?**

A: He was a child of the fifties. All teenagers were into cars then. His love of cars just continued. In some ways they symbolized his success, fit his moods, and seemed to him to be the visible expression that he had made it. He also enjoyed driving. It relaxed him, helped him unwind, think things over, have fun, and like everything else, Elvis took it to the limit. The exhilarating burst of speed on a dark highway was something he really loved.

## *Girls, Relationships, and Priscilla*

**Q: Is it true that Elvis had the sort of temperament that was highly susceptible to love at first sight?**

A: Yes, but it was more like infatuation at first sight. He usually associated love with his first impressions, which was usually infatuation with physical beauty. Elvis had a very precise, perfectionistic ideal of the perfect woman. Bam! Just like that, if he met a girl who fit that image, well, the next thing you knew he was in love and talking about it to anyone who would listen. And love was always associated in his mind with marriage. Marriage was the logical end result of his most passionate, spontaneous encounters. But, like most strong emotions, the urge to marry was not an enduring condition.

The impulse would often fade as soon as the emotion sub-sided. This type of conditional response is most often associated with the immaturity of adolescence. Elvis just never really grew up emotionally. This was unfortunately true about most of his negative character traits.

**Q: One theory some biographers have proposed about Elvis's "love" relationships with women was the "cycle syndrome": (1) love-at-first-sight (2) romantic infatuation leading to marriage talk (3) lessening of infatuation leading to the "play" stages (with the woman taking the initiative in a playful kind of love), and finally (4) the basic role of adoring mother where the woman would mother and pamper Elvis. What is the truth about this theory?**

A: I'm not sure this was true, but even if it were true, the pattern was broken with Priscilla. Her living at Graceland just got her in too deep with Elvis. He never again would commit himself in advance to any girl as he did to Priscilla. Of course, Priscilla was something very special. I have a lot of respect for her.

**Q: Is it true that in his relationships with women Elvis practiced a double standard? That is, he divided women into two groups, "good girls" and "bad girls," and while he could be sexual with "bad girls" he always wanted his "steady" to be a virgin and most especially his future marriage partner to be pure.**

A: Yes. Elvis was in this way like most boys of the fifties. You could play around with "loose" girls, but when it came to marriage, you married a virgin. This was true with Anita Wood, his first serious steady girlfriend and, of course, with Priscilla as she has said in her book *Elvis and Me*. His attitude, however, with his "nonserious" girlfriends was never judgmental.

**Q: Elvis was really old-fashioned when it came to women, wasn't he?**

A: Yes. He didn't like women who smoked, used bad language, drank, or tried to take control of the relationship or criticize him. Pushy or wise-cracking women were a No-No!

**Q: Can you explain why Elvis was so attractive to women?**

A: Simple: Power. Good looks. Charisma. Money. Mystery. Sexy. Sensitive. Strong. Tender. Charming. Provocative. All these come to mind. The hero in any dimestore romance novel usually has some of these traits. Elvis had them all. How could women resist? He was the fantasy of almost every woman.

**Q: In his relationships with girls was Elvis distrustful because he could never be sure whether they were crazy about him or just his public image?**

A: Yes. That also explains his love for Priscilla. She had a way of getting past that distrust. Once Elvis felt a girl liked him for who he was, he could get very compulsive about her. He was really a romantic and, like an adolescent, fell in and out of "infatuation" very easily. But he only really *loved* a few women: Priscilla, Anita Wood, Linda Thompson, Ginger Alden, and, of course, his mother and Lisa Marie.

**Q: Is it true that Elvis was always reticent about approaching new women with whom he might want a relationship?**

A: Elvis was unable to meet new women like most people because of his stardom, so George Klein, a longtime friend of Elvis and a popular figure around Memphis, many times acted as the intermediary between Elvis and his girlfriends. This was true about Anita Wood, Linda Thompson, and Ginger Alden. This was also an area of insecurity for Elvis going back to adolescence, so he made sure it would never happen

again. It is strange that the king of rock 'n' roll, the idol of millions of women, had this fear. Some people never get over the
fear of rejection—adolescent boys in general and Elvis in
particular.

**Q: Could any woman live up to the standards that Elvis
wanted?**

A: No, not really. Elvis himself was never really sure what he
wanted. He also had a tendency to take women for granted
(like men do). Also, the complexity of Elvis's personality
meant that women were often required to play many different roles. Unfortunately, it was always one-sided. Priscilla and
Linda Thompson met Elvis's needs better than any women
in his life.

**Q: Elvis's involvement with Linda Thompson, his girl-
friend from 1972 to 1976, is said to be the most ful-
filling of his life. Is this true?**

A: I'd have to put Priscilla in the same category, but Linda was
an extraordinary woman. She was funny, intelligent, affectionate, and very perceptive about Elvis's needs. No matter
what his moods or demands, Linda had the temperament and
talent to discern them and to satisfy them. Everything was
out front in her relationship with Elvis. There was total trust.
It was the closest relationship he had with any woman except
his mother, Gladys. In fact, Elvis and Linda's relationship was
in many ways like that of a mother and son. Linda was very
"mothering" to Elvis, and they developed a special "baby
talk" language when at times he called her "mommy" and she
called him "Baby Bunting." It was a very affectionate expression of their love for each other. I don't agree with those
people who have tried to psychoanalyze this by saying Elvis
tried to recreate with Linda his relationship with his mother.
Any relationship develops a language all its own; it is in some
ways sacred to that relationship. Sure, Linda "mothered"

him, but what man doesn't need that from time to time? It didn't go on all the time as some have suggested. They had an exceptional relationship.

**Q: Do you think Priscilla's divorcing Elvis hurt his pride more than his heart?**

A: Some writers have said that Elvis didn't really love Priscilla, at least not with a mature love and certainly not in the later years, but in his own way he never stopped loving her. True, his pride was hurt and he was a very vain man, but he never really got over the divorce.

**Q: Did Elvis and Priscilla hold diametrically opposing views on child rearing?**

A: That's a bit too strong a statement. After the divorce, Elvis did what many divorced fathers do when their children visit. He spoiled his daughter. What role guilt over the divorce played in this is pure speculation. But Elvis loved Lisa Marie very much.

**Q: What do you think was really at the heart of Elvis and Priscilla's breakup?**

A: Elvis's lifestyle as an entertainer—his double standard. He wanted Priscilla to stay at home, be content, and always be there for him when he returned home. His concept of being a husband was as protector and provider. Women's roles were very traditional. Elvis, on the other hand, was never able to shake the sense of bachelorhood he had enjoyed for so long. He ran the risk of losing everything he loved because he was not willing to change.

**Q: Did Priscilla know about Elvis's double standard?**

A: Yes, she knew. No one could ever pull the wool over her eyes. She knew everything. She just put up with it, until, I guess, it finally got to her and she'd had enough.

## Religion, Faith, and the Bible

**Q:** **In 1964 Elvis met a new hairdresser, Larry Geller, who introduced him to the literature of the occult and spiritualism. Why do you think Elvis became infatuated with this? Why did he read this type of literature for so long, even committing many passages in those books to memory?**

**A:** Elvis was profoundly religious. In 1964 he became very depressed about his career. He had everything and had indulged in everything and was still empty inside. In short, life had lost its meaning for him. He was at a very vulnerable stage. Also he was not accustomed to calling into question what he perceived to be spiritual truth. This goes back to his childhood. He was taught to respect authority. Larry was very bright and articulate, and this impressed Elvis. But he was a serious seeker after truth all his life—not just in the '60s.

**Q:** **When Elvis traveled on tour, is it true that he carried with him over 200 books dealing with what we'd call today New Age issues? If so, why didn't he take with him any traditional Christian material?**

**A:** Yes, it is true that most of his books would be classified today as New Age, but Elvis also read the Bible regularly. True, he did get far away in his searching from the Christian faith of his boyhood, but he never stopped believing the basics of Christianity, that is, Jesus as God's savior for mankind's sins.

**Q:** **What was Elvis's favorite Bible passage?**

**A:** 1 Corinthians 13. It's called the love chapter of the Bible. When Linda Thompson and Elvis first met, she had verse 13 inscribed on a plaque. It read: "And now these three remain: faith, hope and love. But the greatest of these is love." Elvis's life can best be understood as a "search for love." This plaque is very revealing.

**Q: Can you explain what it was about the New Age-like writings that fascinated Elvis till the last days of his life?**

A: The central teaching in these writings is that God is the voice within us and that we are all, in a manner of speaking, God. External authorities need not concern us. The source of all true spiritual inspiration and wisdom is within ourselves. This idea intrigued Elvis and he found that it explained everything he thought he needed to know. He could now be a teacher or a spiritual adviser to his "followers" without undertaking a systematic, difficult investigation and study. Guided by his "inner light," he was his own authority, which suited his personality and temperament. Coupled with Elvis's religious interest and his current state of emptiness, spiritualism seemed to fill the void. My guess is that if Larry Geller had been a seminary graduate and as well educated in Christian theology and life as he was in spiritualistic doctrine and practices, Elvis would have been just as fascinated with Christian theology and his life would have probably taken a very different direction. Elvis always misunderstood fundamentalist ministers, whom he stereotyped as basically judgmental. This probably goes back to his early career when those ministers led the way in their denunciation of his music and style. In spite of his early exposure to Christianity through the lens of the Assembly of God Church, Elvis knew very little about the Christian faith. From my perspective as a Christian today, I believe Elvis was just in the wrong place at the wrong time and the results were catastrophic for his future as far as his being able to live a happy, productive Christian life. Spiritualism certainly did not give his life purpose and meaning. Once again, emphasis on self appealed to Elvis because he considered himself a self-made man. He overlooked a basic Christian truth contained in the Bible, "I can do all things through Christ who strengthens me."

**Q:** There are several stories written about Elvis's mystical experiences growing out of his immersing himself into the spiritualist literature. How can they be explained?

**A:** Elvis had always been very superstitious, like his mother. The encouragement and fuel of the spiritualistic writings that Larry Geller gave him was like pouring gasoline on a fire. Between 1964 and 1967 a whole series of dramatic visions and voices "visited" themselves on Elvis. Some were as bizarre as his claiming that while listening to a bird, its voice suddenly turned into the voice of Jesus. His early Pentecostal upbringing and biblical illiteracy helped encourage this openness to the supernatural and an uncritical reaction to the power of suggestion. Elvis also believed he was "gifted," chosen by God in a special way. All of this was mixed together in his character to produce exotic behavior. He claimed to be able to read people's minds, lay hands on people to heal them, read the future in someone's palm, make leaves tremble with his "vibes," and much more. Elvis was a very charismatic person and very persuasive. He was compulsive and whenever he got into something new he went all out. His voyage into spiritualism was no different. But he sometimes played games with his beliefs. He often would wink at me after making some grand spiritual pronouncement. I'm not sure how seriously he really took himself. In some ways, everything was a game to Elvis.

**Q:** Some writers have suggested that Elvis often said, especially in the last year of his life, that maybe he should have been a preacher. That he felt he had been "called" years before as a young boy. Is this true?

**A:** As Elvis got more dissatisfied with his life, and boredom set in because he was not fulfilled, he probably got a bit nostalgic or second-guessed himself. Perhaps he had a midlife crisis. He may have reflected on the idea, "If I had it to do over again . . ." Remember, in his experience he thought he had done it all. I think he intuitively knew that there was more to life than materialistic things and occupying his time with increasingly boring activities that he had done a hundred times before. How many cars is enough? He was a virtual prisoner in Graceland. He couldn't go outside the gates without being surrounded by people. He lived an isolated, strange life. Maybe he longed for anonymity, a common celebrity affliction. He may not have been actually serious about this ministerial "call," but yes, I remember him saying wistfully that he wondered if he should have been a preacher. I hope he was sincere because it would have reflected a spark of his original faith.

**Q: Even though Elvis veered away from conventional religion, what Christian beliefs did he continue to hold?**

A: The Trinity, the power of prayer, heaven and hell, the promise of salvation through Jesus Christ. Unfortunately, Elvis was dependent on himself when it came to interpreting the Scriptures and his relationship with the Lord, and his conclusions were often unorthodox. Nevertheless he believed the Bible was the Word of God. He especially liked the Book of Revelation. Within the confines of his isolated life, he remained a deeply spiritual man.

**Q: Was Elvis scared of dying?**

A: No. He was intrigued with death, and his curiosity about the subject led him to study about it. He looked forward to seeing his mom. He actually visited the Memphis city morgue, and believed in confronting the reality of death.

**Q: Several writers have talked about Elvis's tours during the seventies in regal terms like the king before his court, or Elvis as regent. Some have even used religious expressions to describe the performances, using ritualistic terms with Elvis as priest. Is this fair?**

A:  There is no doubt that his fans worshiped him. He was their idol—godlike. He could do no wrong. Even as his performances became more and more perfunctory and he began to gain weight, the fan reaction was always the same. They adored him. So it did become a "ritual" for some of the fans— homage to a monarch or a "communion." Both ideas have some merit.

**Q:  If we could have looked at Elvis while he was alive through God's eyes, what do you think we would have seen?**

A:  The whole message of the Bible is that God is love. I believe God loved Elvis with the same compassion that he loves everyone. I am sure God grieved when Elvis sinned, but God is like the father of the prodigal son—always loving, always waiting for the wayward son to come home, and always waiting with the open arms of forgiveness. My opinion about Elvis's death is based on that kind of love. Some may think it's controversial, and a few critics may have a field day with this, but I believe with all my heart that God saw Elvis's physical and mental suffering and simply brought him home to be with him. That has given me great comfort when I think about Elvis's death.

**Q:  Why do you believe Elvis was a Christian when he lived the way he did?**

A:  My religious tradition teaches once saved always saved. I believe Elvis became a Christian as a young boy. While he may have strayed from the teachings of the church as an adult, his original faith remained safely in the hands of God. I believe my (and Elvis's) faith depends on God's power and faithfulness, not on mine. Some Christian traditions differ on this, but this understanding of the Scripture gives me a strong sense of confidence in Elvis's salvation. Even though Elvis believed many different things concerning the road to salvation, he always came back to the basic biblical teaching that Jesus is God's son who died for our sins and that salvation is through believing this. So while some may say that my strong emotional attachment to Elvis gives me the need to believe that I will see him again in heaven, I feel that my confidence is based on objective evidence and doctrinal belief. When those who share my doctrinal position (and there are millions who do) apply it to Elvis, they come to the same conclusion that I have.

### Drugs, Addiction, and Dependency

**Q: Why did Elvis take drugs?**

A:  At first it was to help keep him awake. Then to help him sleep. In later years, health problems and muscular aches and pains became a convenient excuse. He enjoyed the feeling of relief from pain. Sometimes he would get mad at himself and say, "Man, what am I doing?" But that last year he just didn't care anymore.

**Q: If Elvis had not been an insomniac (and sleepwalker) would he have started taking drugs?**

A:  Perhaps. But the stress of making movies, doing recordings, and his active lifestyle also contributed. Because he sometimes couldn't sleep for days (especially in the sixties) he would approach a manic sleeplessness that eventually required him to take uppers to keep him alert. Then he needed downers to counteract the uppers. He then began compulsively (Elvis never did anything in moderation) to experiment. He bought and practically memorized the *Physicians' Desk Reference* and came to believe he knew more than his doctors about treating his problems. Unfortunately Elvis's tendency of refusing to accept advice or criticism of his judgment increased as he grew older, and I believe eventually led to his death by an overdose of prescription drugs. Elvis got to where nobody could reach him with any message of concern about his behavior. He always thought he knew more and would take advice as criticism, which he couldn't tolerate. Public opinion or even advice from his physicians didn't mean much to him. Because he viewed himself as a "self-made man," he found it difficult to listen to the opinions of others. This trap was set early on, and it carried over into every area of his life.

**Q: How did Elvis justify his deep dependency on prescription drugs?**

A: First, he could never imagine himself a "junkie." Junkies used illegal drugs, while his were prescribed. Second, he had always been an insomniac and really needed medication to help sleep. That's partially how he got started. Third, as he built up a tolerance for the drugs he experimented with, he had to take more and more to get the same effect. Lastly, Elvis lived under enormous and unnatural pressures that— coupled with his continuing drug experiments—began to interfere with his natural functioning and to produce distressing medical problems. The downward spiral continued as his body built up tolerance. His autopsy indicated large doses of several drugs, any one of which would have been lethal to a nonuser, but Elvis took those dosages every day. Remember also that Elvis had a profound capacity for self-delusion and denial.

**Q: Did Elvis ever believe that he was abusing drugs?**

A: No. He thought they were necessary. Since they were technically legal, it was OK for him to take as much as he needed. It's almost as if he said in his mind, "If these drugs could kill me, the government would have made them illegal. So, if I'm careful, I'm safe." And of course, Elvis always felt he was in control of things and knew what was best for himself. But the addict always knows. Deep within, Elvis knew.

**Q: Most Elvis biographers have traced the beginning of his extreme drug, physical, and emotional problems to his learning about Priscilla's infidelity. Would you agree?**

A: To an extent, but Elvis also began his active touring at that time. The emotional trauma of the breakup of his marriage plus the stress and strain of the tour took their toll. True, Priscilla helped keep Elvis in line to a point, and after the divorce there was less accountability. Linda Thompson did a good job, but after that relationship ended it was downhill from there.

**Q: Is it true that sometime around 1972 Elvis's use of drugs escalated beyond control?**

A: Yes, after three years of touring and the lessening of the excitement of the comeback, he began to get bored. Nothing excited him, or any of us for that matter, anymore. In his mind, he had done everything. Elvis hated alcohol, but drugs were already a part of his life. They were just too available to him. Remember also, the divorce occurred about this time. He was then isolated from Lisa Marie. Things just were not turning out the way he had planned. All his wealth wasn't bringing him happiness. He couldn't buy back the love he really needed. He was always, until then, able to buy everything. It's almost as if he felt betrayed by a lifelong philosophy that had suddenly proven empty.

**Q: Was Elvis addicted to drugs in the way the term is understood today to mean "a state of psychic or physical dependence or both on a drug on a continuing basis"?**

A: Yes. I've been "hospitalized" on two occasions and seen many addicts, and I've never seen anybody who could take drugs like Elvis and live through it. He built up an incredible tolerance. The result was a vicious downward spiral that eventually was the cause of his death.

**Q: Why didn't those around Elvis try to stop him, try to tell him he was hurting himself?**

A: Several people made serious attempts. After a while, however, he just didn't want to hear it. He'd say, "Use and abuse are two different things." You just couldn't get through to him. Nobody could talk to him. I tried on several occasions with no success. So did Vernon, Joe Esposito, Jerry Schilling, and Priscilla.

**Q: Did Elvis ever try to dry out?**

A: Yes, on three occasions, once for two weeks in October 1973, once for two weeks in January and February of 1975, and finally two more weeks in August and September of that year. He didn't really cut off completely. Drying out on narcotics and downers is a complicated process, and in Elvis's case it was never more than partially successful. The spiritual dimension was not a part of therapy back then. They spent the time simply getting you off the drugs without addressing the real reason of why you were taking them in the first place.

**Q: Were the fourteen different drugs that were found in Elvis's body after his death normal for Elvis to take before going to bed?**

A: Yes. Over the years Elvis had built up a tolerance for the various prescription drugs he took, especially the ones he needed to get to sleep. He constantly experimented with various combinations and was convinced he knew what was most beneficial for him. A nonuser would probably have died of an overdose if he had taken what Elvis took on a daily basis.

**Q: What has been the greatest benefit to society of Elvis's death?**

A: Elvis's death helped raise the nation's consciousness concerning substance abuse. The prevailing mood in the mid

1970s could be summarized in the phrase "do your own thing." The glamour of the drug culture of the 1960s and '70s came to a screeching halt with Elvis's death. Suddenly, politicians and entertainers alike referred to the tragedy of Elvis's death in their speaking out against drugs. It gave birth to a movement to an extent that exceeded our awareness of drug abuse as it related to the tragic deaths of Janis Joplin, Jimi Hendrix, and Jim Morrison. It was similar to the consciousness raising that followed Rock Hudson's death from AIDS and certainly the current awareness that has been fueled by Magic Johnson's contraction of HIV.

**Q: In your experiences in drug rehabilitation counseling, do you see any similarities between why Elvis became addicted and why those you counsel become addicted?**

A: Obviously there are many circumstances that contribute to someone's becoming an addict. On a psychological level, however, there seems to be one common factor: All addictive behavior is an attempt to deal with unmet needs. Drugs can either substitute for a perceived need or act as a means of numbing the painful feelings that are associated with unmet needs. In Elvis's case I believe his need was to be loved unconditionally and accepted for who he was. His mother was the only person who ever really met that need, and after her death all he had were feelings of emptiness which he tried to numb with prescription drugs. In a way, the drugs became his best friend; they were always there when he needed them and he could depend on them to do what they were supposed to. The drugs never rejected him; they lifted him when he was down; and they put him to sleep. That's about as unconditional as Elvis could find. His problems with drugs weren't related to a lack of will power or an inability to kick the habit; his problem centered on the tyranny of an unmet need—to love and be loved.

## Personality and Temperament

**Q: From a temperament perspective, how can Elvis be described?**

A:  He was at times very manic, highly strung, always behaving as if he were onstage. His violent temper, always only a second away, was unpredictable and inexplicable. He kept everyone on edge. At other times, he could be as quiet and reflective as a monk. He could, especially in his later years, spend days alone in his room. He could also be very loving, compassionate, and sincere. Mood swings were common. As a youngster and up until his late teens, he was very shy and quiet most of the time. Elvis's fans and his being thrust on stage changed him. The performance trap molded him into something complex, confusing, and contradictory. His last two years were more indicative of who Elvis really was inside, behind the performance mask. By then the drugs had him in their grasp and his self-control was gone. He no longer had the ability to really get in touch with who he was, his core personality. In reality, on a less grand and complex scale, all of us are molded by our environment. Elvis's environment was just far more bizarre than the rest of us will ever experience.

**Q: Do you believe that Elvis was really the "rebel without a cause" that he fancied himself and that many of his movies made him out to be?**

A:  No. He was basically not a rebellious personality. He never would stand up to Colonel Parker or anyone else with a strong, self-confident personality who had nothing to lose by standing up to Elvis. The obedient Elvis was always stronger than the rebel Elvis. It was the way he was raised. His anger was always followed by guilt. He had a strong conscience. He was also extremely sensitive to any threat of public dishonor.

**Q:** **It seems that Elvis was a rebel by instinct or image but never by deliberate choice or innate character. Would you agree?**

**A:** Yes. His type of rebellion (dress, talk) never really carried out into overt action. He was always the most naive sort of good citizen. Very patriotic. Very law abiding. Very obedient to anyone he thought his "better." In some ways he always remained that shy, lonely, insecure teenager. Always obedient and compliant to his "elders."

**Q:** **Is it true that Elvis never seemed to enjoy himself unless he was doing something dangerous—tempting fate?**

**A:** I don't think so. Sure, the skating battles at the local roller rink, the daredevil stunts on the roller coaster, racing cars and motorcycles, shooting fireworks all seemed edged with danger. But he enjoyed reading, television, movies, sports, and jamming with friends just as much. It was his way of having fun. He didn't have a death wish.

**Q:** **It's been said that the somewhat violent, reckless things Elvis did were a product of the compulsive behavior that characterized everything he did. How would you explain his self-destructive tendency?**

**A:** Elvis liked to do dangerous things. I don't see this as particularly strange any more than I see the need to explain why people climb mountains with their bare hands or do dangerous stunts. That was just Elvis. I suppose one could speculate and say it was Elvis's way of proving he was no longer a mama's boy or a sissy, but I believe he did what he did simply because he enjoyed it. If he didn't, I don't believe he would have done it just to prove something to others. Of course, there was no one to correct him or keep him in line, and this tended to accentuate some of his little boy antics.

**Q:** **Could you characterize Elvis's behavior as a profoundly self-destructive lifestyle?**

**A:** To a degree both Elvis and I were alike in that we both lived life on the edge. Elvis, however, was aggressive in everything he did. He felt he was living a charmed life and could ride the edge of rational behavior because he was "called" to his vocation. His talent was God-given. He felt he was living a life of destiny. Those who really believe that about themselves behave in ways that most people would call reckless. To Elvis it was normal. Many people have tried to explain his character. The bottom line is that he was predictably spontaneous—a total contradiction. No one will ever be able to explain why Elvis was the way he was. He was an enigma.

**Q:** **Can most of Elvis's behavior prior to his marrying Priscilla be explained as his living out the ideal adolescent fantasy that he felt denied as a shy, unpopular youth—a kind of a postadolescent experience?**

**A:** That's possible. The games he liked to play, the way he related to teenage girls in Memphis during his early years—these were always characterized by a kind of childishness. He really identified with the teen culture. That's probably why he remained so popular with them for so long.

**Q:** **One of Elvis's biographers has described Elvis's personality as one of "menacing sullenness and overbearing arrogance." Is this true?**

**A:** To a certain extent, yes. But what people saw and characterized as arrogance was really his way of masking deep insecurities from his impoverished upbringing and the death of his mother. Elvis never really got over his mother's death. Gladys was the cause of a lot of Elvis's extreme dependency. She was his only confidante and moral conscience. Her death left Elvis confused and adrift emotionally and morally. True, he was very temperamental, but much of his arrogance was part of his image as an entertainer. Sometimes he simply forgot that he wasn't on stage. Those of us who were close to him could see this better than most of his biographers.

**Q: Some people who knew Elvis before and after his army experience say that the army made him "mean." They believe his ugly traits of intimidation and bossing people were exaggerated. Do you support this?**

A: I've heard that, but since I didn't know Elvis before the army I really can't comment personally. I will say that he was a very demanding boss and had a very hot temper. But he was very quick to get over things and try to win back your affection or forgiveness in his usual way. Sometimes he would apologize, but often he would buy you things. Elvis didn't really like relational conflict and had a hard time tolerating any situation for long if he thought someone was upset or displeased with him. He had a deep need to feel loved. He also wanted those around him to know that he loved them, but he had a hard time telling them.

**Q: Was Elvis a manipulative person?**

A: In some ways, yes. But "manipulative" is too strong a word. He didn't really control people out of meanness; he was just determined to get his way. Remember, he was an only child, and Gladys had spoiled him unwittingly. Wealth and fame came early and relatively easy to him. And did he have charm! He really understood what motivated people, and he could do and say just the right thing to get his way. He was also persistent. He got his way sometimes just because he wore the other person down. He persuaded my mother to let me join him on tour when I was only sixteen. But the best example of his power of persuasion was his talking Priscilla's parents into letting her move into Graceland when she was only sixteen years old. Think about that for a moment.

**Q: Did Elvis's moods set the tone for those around him?**

A: Yes. If he was "up," everything was great. But when he was "down," especially in the later years, everyone walked around on eggshells. He could be very unpredictable. But the guys around him were aware of this, and after a while it became comical.

**Q: Can Elvis's complexity be explained in one sense as a war going on inside of him, a war of good vs. bad, or the wild vs. the tame?**

A: Yes, to a certain extent the wildness, spontaneity, and compulsiveness of Elvis was in contradiction to the polite, humble, religious, simple country boy who didn't drink or smoke. Unfortunately, while his fans expected him to be wild on stage, they expected him to be tame at home. It took some sixteen years following his discharge from the army to create the "good" image, so you can imagine the fear Elvis had over the publication of the book *Elvis: What Happened?* This paradox within him caused him to fear the opinion of his fans and at the same time love them. He often said that he knew that everything could be taken away from him just as fast as he got it. It was a very lonely life. "The only time I can really be me," he once said, "is when I walk through that door and lock it on the inside."

**Q: So many negative things have been said about Elvis. Why is that so?**

A: Partially because people think that Elvis was hypocritical—projecting one image to the world but living quite another. There is some truth to that. But let's face it, it's just like the news: Good news doesn't sell papers or get ratings. Positive books aren't controversial, and you need controversy to generate publicity. Also, some people just take pleasure in trying to bring down the mighty or powerful. We are jealous of those who are more wealthy or powerful than ourselves. People take a perverse pleasure in seeing the mighty fall.

**Q: Most men are afraid to show their emotions or share how they are feeling inside. Was Elvis this way?**

A: Not about positive emotions. Elvis felt that there was nothing wrong or nothing to be ashamed of if you show emotions and cry. He was a very sensitive man and often cried over things that touched him. He also shared his feelings regularly. His two traits of sharing his emotions and also being willing to talk about his feelings were more attractive to his girlfriends than his good looks and fame. Women seem drawn to a man like Elvis who is both strong and tender. But he did have difficulty showing negative emotions. He suppressed his anger until it exploded, sometimes at innocent targets. He liked to do things "his way," and that meant he rarely asked for forgiveness.

**Q: Elvis's life would seem to be one of simply "living for the moment." Was he never able to postpone personal gratification?**

A: Usually not. He was like a teenager sometimes in that regard, just a kid in a man's body with all the money and power he could ever need. The sad thing about this is that Elvis thought by being able to buy anything he wanted or controlling those around him who were dependent on him, he had power. In truth, he was powerless. The acts of gross materialism and unpredictable exercise of authority all show the same emptiness and search for love and acceptance. Power without limits is a trap. Power does indeed corrupt and absolute power, with no responsibility or limits, was beyond Elvis's capacity to control. It is, perhaps, beyond anyone's ability.

**Q:** **Most people don't think of Elvis as being a particularly intelligent man. Is that true?**

**A:** He didn't have any formal education beyond high school, but he was shrewd in some things. His musical gifts brought with them a type of intelligence. That has the spark of the divine. His musical memory was extraordinary, and he read extensively, especially dictionaries, where he was always expanding his vocabulary. Medicine, psychology, and philosophy also fascinated him.

**Q:** **Most books about Elvis say he was a classic mama's boy. Is this true?**

**A:** There is no doubt his mother "worshiped" Elvis. He was overly protected as a child. Gladys looked to Elvis for all her emotional support. She spoiled him. He was also kept apart from his relatives and other local children. The result was that the adult Elvis was also spoiled. He expected to be indulged. His ability to tolerate the reclusive nature of his later years may have been encouraged by his "isolated" early relationships with his mother. But considering the amount of abuse many children face, Elvis was very fortunate to have had a loving, protective mother.

**Q:** **Was Elvis as modest about his body as some books have said?**

**A:** Yes. He was very private and hardly ever even allowed himself to be seen in a bathing suit.

**Q:** **Why did Elvis want so many people around him all the time?**

**A:** He was a very social person, but it wasn't really that he needed his friends for his own emotional needs. Everyone had a job to do. Also, with millions of dollars changing hands, he wanted people around who were more than employees, he wanted friends and a sense of family. He often liked to have personal conversations. He liked to talk, and since he really couldn't have a social life in the normal world, his "employees" provided services *and* companionship. This often made it hard on those who worked for him because of the fine line between being a friend and being an employee. This was especially true because Elvis was so emotionally unpredictable.

**Q: What was it about Elvis that made him unique?**

A: He was a nonconformist and had been one all his life. As a child, he was aware that he was different from other children around him. In high school, he was a loner. He dressed and acted differently. He then combined his great vocal gift with this totally unique look and style and literally captured the hearts of an entire generation. To some degree, Elvis can be compared to Madonna. She has shocked society and influenced millions of teenagers, but Elvis didn't use his status as an entertainer to advocate a decadent lifestyle. As Lewis Grizzard once said concerning Elvis, "He may have shook his fanny, but he never showed it."

**Q: Which of Elvis's personality traits do people know the least about?**

A: Without question, people don't know a lot about his sense of humor. He laughed a lot. He especially enjoyed movie comedies; his favorite movies were Blake Edwards's Pink Panther series with Peter Sellers. I don't know how many times we saw Stanley Kubrick's *Dr. Strangelove*. Strangelove's impaired speech and out-of-control right arm always caused Elvis to laugh hysterically. He also enjoyed several of the Monty Python movies. The quick wit and dry, dark, and absurd humor of those British comedians appealed to him. Elvis was also a big practical joker. I especially recall one he played on us one Christmas. All the guys were accustomed to getting bonuses at that time; in fact, we counted on them. Normally, he would just pass out the envelopes containing the bonuses, receive a customary thank you, and move on to the next person. This particular Christmas, however, we had to come to him individually, in private. In a somber tone, he told me that it had been a slow year because he hadn't toured much, he hoped I would understand if the envelope didn't contain the normal "gift." Then he asked me to open it in front of him. When I did, to my shock and dismay (which were compounded by my feeble efforts to show my gratitude), I discovered a McDonald's gift certificate. Of course, the bonuses were eventually distributed, and we were all somewhat amused by all our dramatic performances.

## Fears, Regrets, and the Final Years

**Q: In a word, what was Elvis's basic problem during the last years of his life?**

A: Boredom. Everything got routine for him. There was no challenge. No more dreams to fulfill. He was a revered household word around the world. He was a hero to everyone who counted (in his own world at least). But the boredom was unbearable. He had no goals left. No dreams. He had conquered obstacles but in the process he had trapped himself. He was walled off from any other ways of personal growth.

**Q: Is it true that Elvis had a fear of growing old?**

A: The word "fear" may be too strong, but he did believe that real happiness was only possible in youth. At least when he was younger he felt that way. He was preoccupied with his appearance and often looked for signs of aging, but this is not unusual. Most young people have difficulty picturing middle age as a happy time. He did, however, feel "caught" by the image he thought his fans had of him. He was very concerned about his weight problem in his later years even though this was a trap he had created for himself. His appearance was more important to him than his health.

**Q:** **I've read that Elvis had a fear of losing the talent that had gotten him everything he had. Why do you think he felt that way?**

**A:** Even though Elvis had experienced great material success, he knew it was based on his God-given talent—his singing. He knew (or felt) his fans only loved him for that reason. They didn't really know him. Everyone wants to be loved for *who* they are not *what* they do. He also knew that he didn't really fit anywhere that his talent had taken him. He felt out of place in Hollywood. He knew that some in the pseudo-sophisticated crowd didn't respect him (although many of the great legends of Hollywood did accept him). He felt that if he lost the entertainment business he would be back to driving a truck. Not that he believed that literally, but it was the fear of losing the love and acceptance he thought he'd gained through his singing that most concerned him about losing his talent. His singing had gotten him the attention in the first place.

**Q:** **If Elvis's fatal decline begin with his conflict with Priscilla, why wasn't he able to use this experience to grow personally, to become a stronger, more mature person?**

**A:** Unfortunately, Elvis's personality (or the image that had been so carefully manufactured over the years of the all-conquering man who always got the girls) had him caught in its grasp. Elvis had never known failure of any kind. He never developed the strength that suffering confers on most people throughout their lives. Most of us learn more of the unhappy truth about ourselves and the world at an early age. Elvis's world was never the real world; it was a fantasy world. When the reality of Priscilla's infidelity and divorce finally hit, Elvis couldn't deal with it. Denial was his means of coping, and losing himself in drugs and infantilism was a convenient way to escape.

**Q:** **If during the last few years of Elvis's life the tours exacted a terrible physical toll on him, why didn't he slow down?**

**A:** There were several reasons. First, in the entertainment business, there is a belief that fame is fickle and you better strike while the iron is hot. Also, he felt responsible for all the people who worked for him. Colonel Parker reinforced this belief constantly. In addition, work for Elvis became more and more his only outlet for his problems. Habit and his compulsive take-it-to-the-limit philosophy compelled him to drive himself in this area of his life as it had in every other area. Slowing down would have meant defeat to Elvis, playing it safe. He just didn't live life that way. He would die before slowing down. And he did.

**Q:** **Why didn't someone around Elvis tell him to slow down?**

**A:** No one really wanted to believe Elvis's health was declining. Hindsight is always 20/20, but it just seemed that Elvis was indomitable. Death always seemed distant. Everyone just lived in an unreal world, a magical land that they thought would go on forever. There are thousands of people even today, Elvis's fans, who still don't believe he's dead. That ought to say something about the power of denial. Some thoughts are so terrible that the mind just refuses to think them. The possibility of Elvis's dying was just such a thought to those who were in a totally dependent (and codependent) relationship with him.

**Q:** **Why couldn't Elvis see that his eating habits (high calories and cholesterol, and lots of them) were harmful to him?**

**A:** Back in the early seventies, there was not as much emphasis on health and nutrition as there is today. Very little was being publicized, for example, about the harm of cholesterol.

Elvis loved to eat, and he didn't believe food could hurt him. He had always been able to diet in the past, so he felt that he could if he needed to for some special event (such as the 1973 television special "Aloha from Elvis in Hawaii"). Although, from 1973 on he was less inclined to do so. Anyway, his fans didn't seem to mind. But eating was so much a part of what Elvis liked that nothing could have stopped him from eating what, and how much, he wanted. Besides, as he became more and more bored with life the last two years, eating remained as one of the few pleasures he enjoyed.

**Q: Do you think Elvis, during the last year, was having any guilt or regret about his life?**

A: Yes. With his understanding of the Bible, he probably was having to face the fact that he was not living the kind of life he should have.

**Q: Why were Red and Sonny West fired, especially after Red had been with Elvis for nearly twenty years? In their book, they claim it was a "whim."**

A: Red's temper had resulted in costly lawsuits pending against Elvis. There were regular confrontations between Elvis and Red, and Red and the rest of the group. Red had always rubbed Vernon wrong. Sonny West and Elvis had never gotten along. Financial concerns were also a factor.

**Q: What was the real problem with the book *Elvis: What Happened?* since most of what it says about the facts of Elvis's life have proven to be true?**

A: When revenge and sensationalization are your motives, then you deprive your subject of the dignity that comes with compassion. It revealed and didn't try to explain.

**Q: What effect did the publishing of *Elvis: What Happened?* have on Elvis?**

A:  He was devastated. Had he lived, it could have seriously damaged his career. As it was it destroyed his self-esteem. It crushed his spirit. He was miserable. He really went downhill after hearing about the book. It broke down much of his system of denial. It was finally published fifteen days before Elvis died, but Elvis had acquired a copy of the manuscript several weeks prior to that. Psychologically and emotionally the book made a reality out of Elvis's greatest fear—his image, the Elvis Presley myth, would be tainted. His life and those of everyone who depended on him would never be the same. But before he died, he even found it in his heart to forgive the book's authors—Red West, Sonny West, and Dave Hebler.

Q:  **Why didn't more leak out to the press about Elvis's private life while he was alive?**

A:  Everyone who had regular contact with Elvis (especially family and employees) knew that the one rule you never broke was talking about the Boss to anyone. It was strictly taboo. If you ever did, you knew you'd be fired on the spot.

Q:  **Is it true that Elvis was totally bedridden during the days of his last year?**

A:  Unfortunately, yes. He'd fly into a city and get right into bed as soon as he got there. His crew would have to get him up to do a show. The same was true at Graceland. He very seldom came out of his bedroom.

Q:  **What do you think was Elvis's greatest fear?**

A:  That he'd disappoint his fans. That he could no longer be *the* Elvis Presley.

Q:  **So much has been written about how miserable Elvis was toward the end of his life. Do you believe he was as depressed as some people have said?**

A: Depending on what one is looking for, I would guess that each person around Elvis during those last years has a different opinion of what was going on inside him. Sure, he was bored a lot and his physical problems made him feel bad, but however he was feeling emotionally, he kept it to himself. There were times when things would bother him, but this unhappy, miserable, and angry man that some people have described as Elvis is foreign to me. He was such a little boy at heart, especially early in the morning. We both were. Occasionally, we would catch one of our favorite "Tom and Jerry" cartoons. The unspoken affection we had for each other was something like those cartoon characters, always playing, sometimes mischievous, but always pals at the end. We were a lot like that.

### Memories, Lessons, and Legacy

**Q: One of Elvis's biographers has said that to understand the phenomenon of Elvis, one must take the concept of kingship literally—that Elvis organized his life, performances, friendships, and family around him as if he were literally a "king." How true is this?**

A: There is a case to be made, but it should not be pushed too far. Sure, he certainly lived like a king. So did all of us who traveled with him. Best hotels. Finest foods. True, as Elvis's health deteriorated during the seventies he became more isolated, less accessible. He was a perfectionist about things and so his demands and standards for those who worked for him were high, but not any higher than any demanding employer. What he had was not inherited. He worked very hard for it (unlike a real king) and felt he was thus entitled to spend what he made any way he liked. Also, unlike a real king, he was very aware that his image could be destroyed at any moment—that fans were fickle. About this he was very insecure. I don't think that a real king feels this way.

Elvis's behavior (sleep habits, food, style) can best be described as the compulsive personality of a very insecure man. He wanted desperately to be loved for who and what he really was, and not the "image," but he was afraid if his fans really knew him they would not love him! He was caught in the trap of having created an image people loved, but knowing that was really not him.

**Q: Why is Elvis in some ways "bigger" today than when he was alive?**

A: His phenomenal success in 1956 and 1957 launched Elvis's career. It created so many fans that he could literally make millions off of them for the next twenty years. The same thing was recreated following his death. He was rediscovered. The result was an instant resurrection. Everywhere you turned you saw his face and heard his voice. Never in his life had Elvis's visible presence been so prevalent. Dozens of books were published and his carefully concealed private life was exposed. Curiosity rose to a feverish pitch. More records of Elvis have been sold since his death than he ever sold while he was alive—more than *one billion units* to date. Elvis souvenirs and memorabilia are everywhere. Graceland is a major tourist attraction with more than eight hundred thousand people visiting there each year. Elvis has been replicated in every conceivable form. Mimics, impersonators, and impressionists perform hundreds of times daily around the world. All this combined keeps Elvis "alive." It is not surprising then that controversy surrounding his death would evolve to the point where fanatical fans and opportunistic hucksters labor so hard to prove that he is not even dead. Hence the myth that Elvis staged his own death. It's really a sad commentary on the depths people will go to see their personal needs met.

**Q: Most books about Elvis seem to portray him in extremes, as either a failure or a savior. What's really true?**

A:   Neither. So much has been written that no one can know the "real" Elvis. After a while even Elvis didn't know who he was or what he was. He really was (and certainly now is) bigger than life. Of course, no one can identify with him. These extremes reduce his complexity. He was a very complex man— full of contradictions. Just as soon as you thought you understood him, he'd do something, say something that exploded your conclusions. Either extreme is really inaccurate. This book is written to answer the why questions about Elvis. It tries to be balanced. Like most people, he was both saint and sinner, and God's grace is sufficient to deal with both of those extremes in any person.

Q:   **Is it true that in some ways Elvis was always a lonely, melancholy little boy who spent his life dreaming of all the things he wanted, but when he got them he found that they didn't make him happy?**

A:   Yes. Elvis was always doing things, buying things, giving things away to make himself happy. This behavior seemed to work for years, especially in the sixties. But as Elvis grew older, he found out what most people find out when their lives have been largely the pursuit of pleasure and material things: They don't bring lasting peace of mind and real joy. He failed to realize that true happiness cannot be bought.

Q:   **What do you think is a positive lesson we can learn from Elvis's life?**

A:   Elvis seized the one great opportunity he had in life and made the most of it. But fame is as addictive as any drug, and accountability is needed regardless of who one is. By failing so tragically in many other areas he proved that he was fundamentally no better or worse than any of us. If we make him a saint, we learn nothing from the tragic failures in his life. If we make him an unredeemed sinner, we discount the good of his music, his triumph over abject poverty, his generosity, and his spiritual longings. Balance is the key to appreciating the legacy of Elvis Presley.

**Q:  Can anyone say that they he or she knew Elvis?**

A:  Not really. I knew him as well as anyone. Jerry Schilling and Joe Esposito knew him. Of course Priscilla knew him, although she revealed much of the complexity of Elvis in her book. As soon as you began to think you had him figured out, he'd do something that would totally confuse you. He was a fascinating, complicated man, an enigma—a walking paradox. That's probably the way he wanted it. In some ways he deliberately did things to keep people off guard. Of course, in death the paradox has exploded into legend and myth. By now, I'm not sure anyone would be able to explain the Elvis phenomenon.

**Q:  Of all your memories of life with Elvis, is there one special memory?**

A:  Yes, but it's more a series of memories having to do with the same thing. When Elvis was on tour, one of my responsibilities was to wake him every afternoon at three o'clock. I'd quietly walk into his hotel room (which was almost always adjacent to mine) kneel beside his bed, and then gently place my hand on his shoulder so as not to startle him. I'd whisper, "Elvis, Elvis, it's time to get up," the way a parent might wake a child. Those beautiful blue eyes would begin to blink open slowly. As he began to recognize me, his face would light up in a way that has remained my way of remembering Elvis. The corner of his mouth would turn up, that million-dollar smile would flash, and he'd say, "Nobody can wake me like you, Ricky." It was a simple gift, but it is the most precious memory he ever gave me.

# Epilogue and Acknowledgments

*A*ll in all, I'm at peace with myself and with the Lord. Kent Demerit of *People* magazine said to me, "A good woman will make you better than you are." I've learned that firsthand over the past fourteen years. You see, I married my best friend, Robyn Moye, in 1978. We settled in Fort Walton Beach in the Florida panhandle where we still live with our two beautiful daughters, Brittany and Bethany.

So obviously, my life has changed completely since that day in Pearl, Mississippi—July 3, 1978. I started speaking at hot dog dinners, pizza blasts, and high school events, usually setting up my own sound system in local, area-wide crusades and touring around in an old truck. At the age of twenty-four, I received my high school degree. After attending Criswell Bible College, I went on to earn an associate of divinity degree in 1986 from Southwestern Baptist Theological Seminary.

Since 1978, I've appeared in more than three thousand churches and a thousand high schools throughout the country. I've been on "20/20," "The 700 Club," "PTL," "Tom Snyder," "Good Morning America," "Larry King," "Entertainment Tonight," and "Joan Rivers." Once my story was featured in *People* magazine. Billy Graham has asked me to give my testimony at his crusades on several occasions.

Yet none of this would have been possible without the tremendous help of scores of people along the way. Please indulge me as I offer a humble thank you to these many friends.

I loved the Presley family very much, but they were never able to teach me what my wife's maternal grandparents have. J. B. Mercer taught me about determination, sensitivity, warmth, compassion, and unwavering faith in God. Willa Mercer has stressed prayer and consistency for many years, and her life is a living testament. Genevieve Moye, my mother-in-law, has challenged me more than any other person except my wife, and I love her for it. Her advice concerning her daughter, dealing with the public, and loving my little girls is deeply appreciated. What can I say about her sister Jan Mason? She is a beautiful and godly lady, and her husband, Andy, has an incredible walk with the Lord. Jana, their daughter, is another story in herself. I owe so much to Joe Moye, the closest man in my life since the death of Elvis. I've never known a man with a heart like him. He is the greatest father (and father-in-law) and an even better grandfather. And Granny Moye is a true servant with a big heart; I love you.

To Mom, Billy, and David, whom I love very much. We've been through a lot together.

To Dr. Ike Reighardt for teaching me how to express love as a man to other people; Al Holley helped, too . . . Dr. Jay Strack for listening and relating . . . Dr. Freddie Gage for recognizing my call . . . Dr. and Mrs. W. A. Criswell for the scholarship to college and encouragement . . . Dr. Paige Patterson for adding sound learning scholarship to my calling . . . Drs. Richard and Becky Land for their teaching on counseling and the home . . . Dr. Charles Carter and his lessons on ethics . . . Rev. Aubry Edwards and Richie Kingsmore for their emphasis on music . . . David, Lagene, Davy, Nicki, and Eli Akin for becoming the new brothers and sister I thought could not be replaced. I was wrong . . . Dr. James Meritt for his mind and granitelike jaw . . . Dr. Don LaBelle and Pat LaBelle, my pastor and his wife, for their counsel and prayers . . . Danny, Mark, Teresa, Doug, Pam, and the members of Wright Baptist Church for being the family of God to our family . . . Dr. and Mrs. James Monroe, two godly people I love and respect . . . The professors at Southwestern Baptist Theological Seminary in Fort Worth, Texas; especially

Drs. Curtis Vaught, Bruce Corley (a widower who never quit at home), and Jack McGorman (he lost his son that year) . . . To the many student ministers across the nation . . . To name a few: Rick Caldwell, Larry Betrand, Hugh ("Huge") Kirby, Johnny Derouen . . . To all the pastors and friends in churches where I have spoken . . . To my father, Bill, and his wife Lois (I'm so glad we had a chance to become close. I'll see you in heaven, Daddy) . . . Mrs. Gay McRae (the greatest Elvis fan in the world) . . . Joe Esposito and Jerry Shilling (I love you both and appreciate your friendship through the years) . . . Greg Menze, Dave Sundee, Skip Tshirtman, Janice and Chester Caruthers (our prayer partners) . . . The Kalla Family, Benny and Marylou, Syndee Rose, John and Susie Bell, Kim and Steve and Missy, David Nassar, Mark and Todd Roberts, Larry Noe, Buddy and Judy Gibbs, Connie and Earl Duggins, Greg Davidson, Rev. Lewis Staton and the Maranatha Baptist Church, Rob Mullins, Dr. Adrian Rogers, Rod and Cindy Smith, Aunt Mary Gene and Uncle Rip, Jim and Joey Wilson, Michael and Terry Boccia, Tim and Ann Marie Jibson, Lee Mabry, Jerome and Freda Olds, and the boys . . . Joey Paul at Word for his patience, persistence, and prayer, and the people at Word for believing that I had a story worth telling . . . Mylon LeFevre for being the first to call after Elvis died . . . Dr. Jerry Falwell and the students at Liberty . . . Dr. Billy Graham and his wife, Ruth, for keeping the standard high.

Last and most importantly, I owe everything to Jesus Christ, my Savior and Lord. He saved me and put my feet on solid ground and gave me a life worth living. For all of this and more I will be grateful for all eternity.

# Appendixes

## *Albums*

April 1956       Elvis Presley
Blue Suede Shoes, I'm Counting on You, I Got a Woman, One-Sided Affair, I Love You Because, Just Because, Tutti Frutti, Tryin' to Get to You, I'm Gonna Sit Right Down and Cry, I'll Never Let You Go, Blue Moon, Money Honey
RCA LSP 1254

October 1956      Elvis
Rip It Up, Love Me, When My Blue Moon Turns to Gold Again, Long Tall Sally, First in Line, Paralyzed, So Glad You're Mine, Old Shep, Ready Teddy, Anyplace Is Paradise, How's the World Treating You, How Do You Think I Feel?
RCA LSP 1382

July 1957      Loving You
From the film: Mean Woman Blues, Teddy Bear, Loving You, Got a Lot o' Lovin' to Do, Lonesome Cowboy, Hot Dog, Party. Bonus songs: Blueberry Hill, True Love, Don't Leave Me Now, Have I Told You Lately That I Love You? I Need You So
RCA LSP 1515

November 1957      Elvis's Christmas Album
Santa Claus Is Back in Town, White Christmas, Here Comes Santa Claus, I'll Be Home for Christmas, Blue Christmas, Santa Bring My Baby Back, O Little Town of Bethlehem, Silent Night, Peace in the Valley, Believe, Take My Hand, Precious Lord, It Is No Secret
RCA LSP 1035

March 1958      Elvis's Golden Records
Hound Dog, Loving You, All Shook Up, Heartbreak Hotel, Jailhouse Rock, Love Me, Too Much, Don't Be Cruel, That's When Your Heartaches Begin, Teddy Bear, Love Me Tender, Treat Me Nice, Any Way You Want Me, I Want You, I Need You, I Love You
RCA LSP 1707

August 1958         King Creole
     King Creole, As Long As I Have You, Hard Headed Woman, Trouble,
     Dixieland Rock, Don't Ask Me Why, Lover Doll, Crawfish, Young
     Dreams, Steadfast, Loyal and True, New Orleans
                                                    RCA LSP 1884


February 1959         For LP Fans Only
     That's All Right, Lawdy, Miss Clawdy, Mystery Train, Poor Boy, Play-
     ing for Keeps, My Baby Left Me, I Was the One, Rattle and Roll,
     You're a Heartbreaker, I'm Left, You're Right, She's Gone
                                                    RCA LSP 1990


August 1959         A Date with Elvis
     Blue Moon of Kentucky, Young and Beautiful, Baby, I Don't Care,
     Milkcow Blues Boogie, Baby, Let's Play House, Good Rockin' To-
     night, Is It So Strange? We're Gonna Move, I Want to Be Free, I For-
     got to Remember to Forget
                                                    RCA LSP 2011


December 1959         50,000,000 Elvis Fans Can't Be Wrong
                      Elvis's Gold Records, Vol. 2
     A Fool Such As I, I Need Your Love Tonight, Wear My Ring Around
     Your Neck, Doncha' Think It's Time, I Beg of You, A Big Hunk o'
     Love, Don't, My Wish Came True, One Night, I Got Stung
                                                    RCA LSP 2075


April 1960         Elvis Is Back
     Fever, Girl Next Door Went-a-Walking, Soldier Boy, Make Me Know
     It, I Will Be Home Again, Reconsider, Baby, It Feels So Right, Like a
     Baby, The Girl of My Best Friend, Thrill of Your Love, Such a Night,
     Dirty Feeling
                                                    RCA LSP 2231


October 1960         G.I. Blues
     Tonight Is So Right for Love, What's She Really Like? Frankfurt Spe-
     cial, Wooden Heart, G.I. Blues, Pocketful of Rainbows, Shoppin'
     Around, Big Boots, Didja' Ever, Blue Suede Shoes, Doin' the Best I
     Can
                                                    RCA LSP 2256

December 1960     His Hand in Mine
His Hand in Mine, I'm Gonna Walk Dem Golden Stairs, In My Father's House, Milky White Way, Known Only to Him, I Believe in the Man in the Sky, Joshua Fit the Battle, Jesus Knows What I Need, Swing Down, Sweet Chariot, Mansion over the Hilltop, If We Never Meet Again, Working on the Building
RCA LSP 2328

June 1961     Something for Everbody
The Ballad Side: There's Always Me, Give Me the Right, It's a Sin, Sentimental Me, Starting Today, Gently. The Rhythm Side: I'm Comin' Home, In Your Arms, Put the Blame on Me, Judy, I Want You with Me. Bonus songs: I Slipped, I Stumbled, I Fell (from *Wild in the Country*)
RCA LSP 2370

October 1961     Blue Hawaii
Blue Hawaii, Almost Always True, Aloha Oe, No More, Can't Help Falling in Love, Rock-a-Hula Baby, Moonlight Swim, Ku-u-i-po, Ito Eats, Slicin' Sand, Hawaiian Wedding Song
RCA LSP 2436

June 1962     Pot Luck
Kiss Me Quick, Just for Old Times' Sake, Gonna Get Back Home Somehow, Easy Question, Steppin' Out of Line (from *Blue Hawaii*), I'm Yours, Something Blue, Suspicion, I Feel That I've Known You Forever, Night Rider, Fountain of Love, That's Someone You Never Forget
RCA LSP 2523

November 1962     Girls! Girls! Girls!
Girls! Girls! Girls! I Don't Wanna Be Tied, Where Do You Come From? I Don't Want To, We'll Be Together, A Boy Like Me, a Girl Like You, Earth Boy, Return to Sender, Because of Love, Thanks to the Rolling Sea, Song of the Shrimp, The Walls Have Ears, We're Coming in Loaded
RCA LSP 2621

March 1963     It Happened at the World's Fair
Beyond the Bend, Relax, Take Me to the Fair, They Remind Me Too Much of You, One Broken Heart for Sale, I'm Falling in Love Tonight,

Cotton Candy Land, A World of Our Own, How Would You Like to Be? Happy Ending

RCA LSP 2697

September 1963      Elvis's Golden Records, Vol. 3
It's Now or Never, Stuck on You, Fame and Fortune, I Gotta Know, Surrender, I Feel So Bad, Are You Lonesome Tonight? His Latest Flame, Little Sister, Good Luck Charm, Anything That's Part of You, She's Not You

RCA LSP 2765

November 1963      Fun in Acapulco
Fun in Acapulco, Vino, Dinero y Amor, Mexico, El Toro, Marguerita, The Bullfighter Was a Lady, No Room to Rhumba in a Sports Car, I Think I'm Gonna Like It Here, Bossa Nova Baby, You Can't Say No in Acapulco, Guadalajara. Bonus songs: Love Me Tonight, Slowly But Surely

RCA LSP 2756

March 1964      Kissin' Cousins
Kissin' Cousins, Smokey Mountain Boy, There's Gold in the Mountains, One Boy, Two Little Girls, Catchin' On Fast, Tender Feeling, Anyone, Barefoot Ballad, Once Is Enough. Bonus songs: Echoes of Love, Long, Lonely Highway

RCA LSP 2894

October 1964      Roustabout
Roustabout, Little Egypt, Poison Ivy League, Hard Knocks, It's a Wonderful World, Big Love, Big Heartache, One-Track Heart, It's Carnival Time, Carny Town, There's a Brand New Day on the Horizon, Wheels on My Heels

RCA LSP 2999

April 1965      Girl Happy
Girl Happy, Spring Fever, Fort Lauderdale Chamber of Commerce, Startin' Tonight, Wolf Call, Do Not Disturb, Cross My Heart and Hope to Die, The Meanest Girl in Town, Do the Clam, Puppet on a String, I've Got to Find My Baby. Bonus song: You'll Be Gone

RCA LSP 3338

July 1965          Elvis for Everyone
Your Cheatin' Heart, Summer Kisses, Winter Tears, Finders Keepers, Losers Weepers, In My Way (from *Wild in the Country*), Tomorrow Night, Memphis, Tennessee, For the Millionth and the Last Time, Forget Me Never (from *Wild in the Country*), Sound Advice (from *Follow That Dream*), Santa Lucia (from *Viva Las Vegas*), I Met Her Today, When It Rains, It Really Pours
RCA LSP 3450

October 1965          Harum Scarum
Harem Holiday, My Desert Serenade, Go East—Young Man, Mirage, Kismet, Shake That Tambourine, Hey Little Girl, Golden Coins, So Close, Yet So Far. Bonus songs: Animal Instinct, Wisdom of the Ages
RCA LSP 3468

April 1965          Frankie and Johnny
Frankie and Johnny, Come Along, Petunia, the Gardener's Daughter, Chesay, What Every Woman Lives For, Look Out, Broadway, Beginner's Luck, Down by the Riverside and When the Saints Go Marching In (medley), Shout It Out, Hard Luck, Please Don't Stop Loving Me, Everybody Come Aboard
RCA LSP 3553

June 1965          Paradise: Hawaiian Style
Paradise: Hawaiian Style, Queenie Wahine's Papaya, Scratch My Back, Drums of the Islands, Datin', A Dog's Life, House of Sand, Stop Where You Are, This Is My Heaven. Bonus song: Sand Castles
RCA LSP 3643

October 1966          Spinout
Stop, Look and Listen, Adam and Evil, All That I Am, Never Say Yes, Am I Ready, Beach Shack, Spinout, Smorgasbord, I'll Be Back. Bonus songs: Tomorrow Is a Long Time, Down in the Alley, I'll Remember You
RCA LSP 3702

March 1967          How Great Thou Art
How Great Thou Art, In the Garden, Somebody Bigger Than You and I, Farther Along, Stand by Me, Without Him, So High, Where Could I Go But to the Lord, By and By, If the Lord Wasn't Walking

by My Side, Run On, Where No One Stands Alone, Crying in the
Chapel

RCA LSP 3758

June 1967          Double Trouble
Double Trouble, Baby, If You'll Give Me All of Your Love, Could I Fall
in Love, Long Legged Girl, City by Night, Old MacDonald, I Love Only
One Girl, There Is So Much World to See. Bonus songs: It Won't Be
Long, Never Ending, Blue River, What Now, What Next, Where To?

RCA LSP 3787

November 1967     Clambake
Clambake, Who Needs Money, A House That Has Everything, Con-
fidence, Hey, Hey, Hey, You Don't Know Me, The Girl I Never Loved.
Bonus songs: Guitar Man, How Can You Lose What You Never Had?
Big Boss Man, Singing Tree, Just Call Me Lonesome

RCA LSP 3893

February 1968     Elvis's Gold Records, Vol. 4
Love Letters, Witchcraft, It Hurts Me, What'd I Say, Please Don't
Drag That String Around, Indescribably Blue, You're the Devil in
Disguise, Lonely Man, A Mess of Blues, Ask Me, Ain't That Loving
You, Baby, Just Tell Her Jim Said Hello

RCA LSP 3921

June 1968          Speedway
Speedway, There Ain't Nothing Like a Song (with Nancy Sinatra),
Your Time Hasn't Come Yet Baby, Who Are You? He's Your Uncle,
Not Your Dad, Let Yourself Go, Your Groovy Self (with Nancy
Sinatra). Bonus song: Five Sleepy Heads, Western Union, Mine,
Goin' Home, Suppose

RCA LSP 3989

November 1968     Elvis Singing Flaming Star and Others
Flaming Star (from *Flaming Star*), Wonderful World (from *Live a
Little, Love a Little*), Night Life, All I Needed Was the Rain, Too Much
Monkey Business, Yellow Rose of Texas and The Eyes of Texas
(medley), She's a Machine, Do the Vega, Tiger Man (recorded live
at NBC for the Elvis special for which this album was released
through Singer Sewing Centers)

RCA PRS 279

December 1968      Elvis (TV Special)
Trouble and Guitar Man, Lawdy, Miss Clawdy and Baby, What You Want Me to Do, Dialogue, Medley: Heartbreak Hotel, Hound Dog, All Shook Up, Can't Help Falling in Love, Jailhouse Rock, Dialogue, Love Me Tender, Dialogue, Where Could I Go But to the Lord, Up Above My Head and Saved, Dialogue, Blue Christmas, Dialogue, One Night, Memories, Medley: Nothingville, Dialogue, Big Boss Man, Guitar Man, Little Egypt, Trouble, Guitar Man, If I Can Dream

RCA LPM 4088

April 1969      Elvis Sings "Flaming Star"
Commercial release of Elvis's album (RCA PRS–279) issued as a special premium in November 1968 in conjunction with the Singer television program.

RCA CAS–2304

May 1969      From Elvis in Memphis
Wearin' That Loved On Look, Only the Strong Survive, I'll Hold You in My Heart, Long Black Limousine, It Keeps Right on A-Hurtin', I'm Movin' On, Power of My Love, Gentle on My Mind, After Loving You, True Love Travels on a Gravel Road, Any Day Now, In the Ghetto

RCA LSP 4155

November 1969      From Memphis to Vegas/From Vegas to Memphis
(2–record set)
Blue Suede Shoes, Johnny B. Goode, All Shook Up, Are You Lonesome Tonight? Hound Dog, I Can't Stop Loving You, My Babe, Mystery Train and Tiger Man (medley), Words, In the Ghetto, Suspicious Minds, Can't Help Falling in Love, Inherit the Wind, This Is the Story, Stranger in My Own Home Town, A Little Bit of Green, And the Grass Won't Pay No Mind, Do You Know Who I Am? From a Jack to a King, The Fair's Moving On, You'll Think of Me, Without Love

RCA LSP 6020

April 1970      Let's Be Friends
Stay Away, Joe (from *Stay Away, Joe*), If I'm a Fool, Let's Be Friends, Let's Forget About the Stars, Mama (from *Girls! Girls! Girls!*), I'll Be There, Almost (from *The Trouble with Girls*), Change of Habit (from *Change of Habit*), Have a Happy (from *Change of Habit*)

RCA CAS–2408

May 1970        On Stage: February 1970
> See See Rider, Release Me, Sweet Caroline, Run-away, The Wonder of You, Polk Salad Annie, Yesterday, Proud Mary, Walk a Mile in My Shoes, Let It Be Me
>
>                               RCA LSP 4362

August 1970       Worldwide 50 Gold Award Hits, Vol. 1
> Heartbreak Hotel, I Was the One, I Need You, I Love You, Don't Be Cruel, Hound Dog, Love Me Tender, Any Way You Want Me, Too Much, Playing for Keeps, All Shook Up, That's When Your Heartaches Begin, Loving You, Teddy Bear, Jailhouse Rock, Trust Me Nice, I Beg of You, Don't, Wear My Ring Around Your Neck, Hard Headed Woman, I Got Stung, A Fool Such As I, A Big Hunk o' Love, Stuck on You, A Mess of Blues, It's Now or Never, I Gotta Know, Are You Lonesome Tonight? Surrender, I Feel So Bad, Little Sister, Can't Help Falling in Love, Rock-a-Hula Baby, Anything That's Part of You, Good Luck Charm, She's Not You, Return to Sender, Where Do You Come From? One Broken Heart for Sale, The Devil in Disguise, Bossa Nova Baby, Kissin' Cousins, Viva Las Vegas, Ain't That Loving You, Baby, Wooden Heart, Crying in the Chapel, If I Can Dream, In the Ghetto, Suspicious Minds, Don't Cry, Daddy, Kentucky Rain. Plus excerpts from *Elvis Sails*
>
>                               RCA LPM 6401

November 1970     Back in Memphis
> Inherit the Wind, This Is the Story, Stranger in My Own Home Town, A Little Bit of Green, The Grass Won't Pay No Mind, Do You Know Who I Am? From a Jack to a King, The Fair's Moving On, You'll Think of Me, Without Love
>
>                               RCA LSP 4429

November 1970     Elvis's Christmas Album
> Blue Christmas, Silent Night, White Christmas, Santa Claus Is Back in Town, I'll Be Home for Christmas, If Every Day Was Like Christmas, Here Comes Santa Claus, O Little Town of Bethlehem, Santa Bring My Baby Back, Mama Like the Roses
>
>                               RCA CAL–2428

November 1970     Almost in Love
> Almost in Love (from *Live a Little, Love a Little*), Long Legged Girl (from *Double Trouble*), Edge of Reality (from *Live a Little, Love a*

*Little*), My Little Friend, A Little Less Conversation (from *Live a Little, Love a Little*), Rubberneckin' (from *Change of Habit*), Clean Up Your Own Back Yard (from *The Trouble with Girls*), U.S. Male (from *Stay Away, Joe*), Charro! (from *Charro!*), Stay Away, Joe (from *Stay Away, Joe*)

RCA CAS–2440

December 1970     Elvis: That's the Way It Is
I Just Can't Help Believin', Twenty Days and Twenty Nights, How the Web Was Woven, Patch It Up, Mary in the Morning, You Don't Have to Say You Love Me, You've Lost That Lovin' Feeling, I've Lost Me, You've Lost That Lovin' Feeling, I've Lost You, Just Pretend, Stranger in the Crowd, The Next Step Is Love, Bridge over Troubled Water

RCA LSP 4445

March 1971     You'll Never Walk Alone
You'll Never Walk Alone, Who Am I? Let Us Pray (from *Change of Habit*), (There'll Be) Peace in the Valley, We Call on Him, I Believe, It Is No Secret (What God Can Do), Sing You Children, Take My Hand, Precious Lord

RCA CALX–2472

March 1971     Elvis Country
Snowbird, Tomorrow Never Comes, Little Cabin on the Hill, Whole Lotta Shakin' Goin' On, Funny How Time Slips Away, I Really Don't Want to Know, There Goes My Everything, It's Your Baby, You Rock It, The Fool, Faded Love, I Washed My Hands in Muddy Water, Make the World Go Away, I Was Born About Ten Thousand Years Ago

RCA LSP 4460

August 1971     Love Letters from Elvis
Love Letters, When I'm Over You, If I Were You, Got My Mojo Working, Heart of Rome, Only Believe, This Is Our Dance, Cindy, Cindy, I'll Never Know, Life, It Ain't No Big Thing

RCA LSP 4530

August 1971     C'mon Everybody
C'mon Everybody, Angel, Easy Come, Easy Go, A Whistling Tune, Follow That Dream, King of the Whole Wide World, I'll Take Love, Today, Tomorrow and Forever, I'm Not the Marrying Kind, This Is Living

RCA CAL–2518

September 1971      Elvis: The Other Sides—
                   Worldwide Gold Award Hits, Vol. 2
Puppet on a String, Witchcraft, Poor Boy, I Want to Be Free, Doncha'
Think It's Time, Young Dreams, The Next Step Is Love, You Don't
Have to Say You Love Me, Paralyzed, My Wish Came True, When
My Blue Moon Turns to Gold Again, Lonesome Cowboy, My Baby
Left Me, It Hurts Me, I Need Your Love Tonight, Tell Me Why, Please
Don't Drag That String Around, Young and Beautiful, Hot Dog, New
Orleans, We're Gonna Move, Crawfish, King Creole, I Believe in the
Man in the Sky, Dixieland Rock, The Wonder of You, They Remind
Me Too Much of You, Mean Woman Blues, Lonely Man, Any Day
Now, Don't Ask Me Why, Marie's the Name—His Latest Flame, I
Really Don't Want to Know, (You're So Square) Baby I Don't Care,
I've Lost You, Let Me, Love Me, Got a Lot o' Living to Do, Fame and
Fortune, Rip It Up, There Goes My Everything, Lover Doll, One
Night, Just Tell Her Jim Said Hello, Ask Me, Patch It Up, As Long As
I Have You, You'll Think of Me, Wild in the Country
                                            RCA LPM 6402


November 1971      I Got Lucky
I Got Lucky (from *Kid Galahad*), What a Wonderful Life (from *Follow That Dream*), I Need Somebody to Lean On (from *Viva Las Vegas*), Yoga Is As Yoga Does (from *Easy Come, Easy Go*), Riding the
Rainbow (from *Kid Galahad*), Fools Fall in Love, The Love Machine
(from *Easy Come, Easy Go*), Home Is Where the Heart Is (from *Kid Galahad*), You Gotta Stop (from *Easy Come, Easy Go*), If You Think I
Don't Need You (from *Viva Las Vegas*)
                                            RCA CAL–2533


December 1971      The Wonderful World of Christmas
O Come, All Ye Faithful, The First Noel, Winter Wonderland, Silver
Bells, On a Snowy Christmas Night, It Won't Seem Like Christmas,
I'll Be Home on Christmas Day, Holly Leaves and Christmas Trees,
Merry Christmas Baby, If I Get Home on Christmas Day, The Wonderful World of Christmas
                                            RCA LSP 4579


March 1972         Elvis—Now
Help Me Make It Through the Night, Miracle of the Rosary, Hey
Jude, Put Your Hand in the Hand, Until It's Time for You to Go, We
Can Make the Morning, Early Mornin' Rain, Sylvia, Fools Rush In, I
Was Born Ten Thousand Years Ago
                                            RCA LSP 4671

March 1972          Elvis Sings Hits from His Movies, Vol. 1
Down by the Riverside and When the Saints Go Marching In (from *Frankie and Johnny*), They Remind Me Too Much of You (from *It Happened at the World's Fair*), Confidence (from *Clambake*), Frankie and Johnny (from *Frankie and Johnny*), Guitar Man, Long Legged Girl (With the Short Dress On) (from *Double Trouble*), You Don't Know Me (from *Clambake*), How Would You Like to Be (from *It Happened at the World's Fair*), Big Boss Man, Old MacDonald (from *Double Trouble*)

RCA CAS–2567

June 1972          He Touched Me
He Touched Me, I've Got Confidence, Amazing Grace, Seeing Is Believing, He Is My Everything, Bosom of Abraham, An Evening Prayer, Lead Me, Guide Me, There Is No God But God, A Thing Called Love, I, John, Reach Out to Jesus

RCA LSP 4690

July 1972          "Burning Love" and Hits from His Movies, Vol. 2
Burning Love, Tender Feeling, Am I Ready? Tonight Is So Right for Love, Guadalajara, It's a Matter of Time, No More, Santa Lucia, We'll Be Together, I Love Only One Girl

RCA CAS–2595

August 1972          Elvis As Recorded Live at Madison Square Garden
                     (June 10, 1972)
Introduction: Also Sprach Zarathustra, That's All Right, Proud Mary, Never Been to Spain, You Don't Have to Say You Love Me, You've Lost That Lovin' Feelin', Polk Salad Annie, Love Me, All Shook Up, Heartbreak Hotel, Medley: (Let Me Be Your) Teddy Bear and Don't Be Cruel, Love Me Tender, The Impossible Dream, Introductions by Elvis, Hound Dog, Suspicious Minds, For the Good Times, American Trilogy, Funny How Time Slips Away, I Can't Stop Loving You, Can't Help Falling in Love

RCA LSP 4776

November 1972     Separate Ways
Separate Ways, Sentimental Me, In My Way, I Met Her Today, What Now, What Next, Where To, Always on My Mind, I Slipped, I Stumbled, I Fell, Is It So Strange, Forget Me Never, Old Shep

RCA CAS–2611

April 1973          Aloha from Hawaii via Satellite (January 14, 1973)
Introduction: Also Sprach Zarathustra, See See Rider, Burning Love,
Something, You Gave Me a Mountain, Steamroller Blues, My Way,
Love Me, Johnny B. Goode, It's Over, Blue Suede Shoes, I'm So Lone-
some I Could Cry, I Can't Stop Loving You, Hound Dog, What Now
My Love, Fever, Welcome to My World, Suspicious Minds, Introduc-
tions by Elvis, I'll Remember You, Medley: Long Tall Sally and Whole
Lotta Shakin' Goin' On, American Trilogy, A Big Hunk o' Love, Can't
Help Falling in Love
                                        RCA VPSX–6089

July 1973          Elvis
Fool, Where Do I Go from Here, It's Impossible, It's Still Here, I Will
Be True, I'll Take You Home Again Kathleen, (That's What You Get)
For Lovin' Me, Padre, Don't Think Twice, It's All Right, Love Me,
Love the Life I Lead
                                        RCA APL 1–0283

October 1973          Raised on Rock/For Ol' Times' Sake
Raised on Rock, Are You Sincere, Find Out What's Happening, I Miss
You, Girl of Mine, For Ol' Times' Sake, If You Don't Come Back, Just
a Little Bit, Sweet Angeline, Three Corn Patches
                                        RCA APL 1–0388

January 1974          ELVIS: A Legendary Performer, Vol. 1
That's All Right, I Love You Because (unreleased take), Heartbreak
Hotel, Don't Be Cruel, Love Me (unreleased live version), Trying to
Get to You (unreleased live version), Love Me Tender, (There'll Be)
Peace in the Valley, (Now and Then There's) A Fool Such As I,
Tonight's All Right for Love (unreleased song from *G.I. Blues*), Are
You Lonesome Tonight? (unreleased live version), Can't Help Falling
in Love, plus excerpts from Elvis's press conference on September
22, 1958
                                        RCA CPL 1–0341

May 1974          Good Times
Take Good Care of Her, Loving Arms, I Got a Feelin' in My Body, If
That Isn't Love, She Wears My Ring, I've Got a Thing About You
Baby, My Boy, Spanish Eyes, Talk About the Good Times, Good
Time Charlie's Got the Blues
                                        RCA CPL 1–0475

September 1974     Elvis As Recorded Live on Stage in Memphis
See See Rider, I Got a Woman, Love Me, Trying to Get to You, Medley: Long Tall Sally, Whole Lotta Shakin' Goin' On, Flip, Flop and Fly, Jailhouse Rock and Hound Dog, Why Me Lord? How Great Thou Art, Medley: Blueberry Hill and I Can't Stop Loving You, Help Me, An American Trilogy, Let Me Be There, My Baby Left, Lawdy, Miss Clawdy, Can't Help Falling in Love
RCA CPL–0606

October 1974     Having Fun with Elvis on Stage
A talking album only—Elvis talking to and with his concert audiences (album was privately recorded and marketed briefly before RCA purchased the rights).
RCA CPM 1–0818

January 1975     Promised Land
Promised Land, There's a Honky Tonk Angel (Who Will Take Me Back In), Help Me, Mr. Songman, Love Song of the Year, It's Midnight, Your Love's Been a Long Time Coming, If You Talk in Your Sleep, Thinking About You, You Asked Me To
RCA APL 1–0873

January 1976     ELVIS: A Legendary Performer, Vol. 2
Harbor Lights (unreleased Sun recording), How Great Thou Art, If I Can Dream, I Want You, I Need You, I Love You (unreleased alternate take), Blue Christmas, Blue Suede Shoes (unreleased live recording), It's Now or Never, Blue Hawaii (unreleased live recording), Jailhouse Rock, 1956 interview, Such a Night, Blue Hawaii (unreleased live recording), 1961 awards presentation to Elvis, Cane and a High Starched Collar (unreleased recording)
RCA CPL 1–1349

April 1975     Elvis: Pure Gold
Love Me Tender, Loving You, Kentucky Rain, Fever, It's Impossible, Jailhouse Rock, Don't Be Cruel, I Got a Woman, All Shook Up, In the Ghetto
ANL 1–0971

March 1976     ELVIS: The Sun Sessions
That's All Right, Blue Moon of Kentucky, I Don't Care If the Sun Don't Shine, Good Rockin' Tonight, Milkcow Blues Boogie, You're a

Heartbreaker, I'm Left, You're Right, She's Gone, Baby Let's Play House, Mystery Train, I Forgot to Remember to Forget, I'll Never Let You Go, I Love You Because (first version), I Love You Because (second version), Blue Moon, Trying to Get to You, Just Because

RCA APM 1–1675

May 1976           From Elvis Presley Boulevard, Memphis, Tennessee
                         (Recorded Live)
Hurt, Never Again, Blue Eyes Crying in the Rain, Danny Boy, The Last Farewell, For the Heart, Better They Are, Harder They Fall, Love Coming Down, I'll Never Fall in Love Again

RCA APL 1–1506

March 1977        Welcome to My World
Welcome to My World (live recording), Help Me Make It Through the Night, Release Me (and Let Me Love Again) (live recording), I Really Don't Want to Know, For the Good Times (live recording), Gentle on My Mind, Make the World Go Away (live recording), Your Cheatin' Heart, I'm So Lonesome I Could Cry (live recording), I Can't Stop Loving You (previously released live recording)

RCA APL 1–2274

June 1977          Moody Blue
Moody Blue, She Thinks I Still Care, Way Down, Pledging My Love, It's Easy for You, Let Me Be There, If You Love Me Let Me Know, He'll Have to Go, Unchained Melody, Little Darlin'

RCA AFL 1–2428

## *Top-Ten Hits*

| | Recording Date | Chart Debut | Peak Chart Position |
|---|---|---|---|
| Heartbreak Hotel (M. Axton, T. Durden, E. Presley) | 1–10–56 | 3–3–56 | 1 |
| I Want You, I Need, I Love You (M. Mysels, I. Kosloff) | 4–11–56 | 5–26–56 | 1 |
| Hound Dog (J. Leiber, M. Stoller) | 7–2–56 | 8–4–56 | 1 |
| Don't Be Cruel (O. Blackwell, E. Presley) | 7–2–56 | 8–4–56 | 1 |
| Love Me Tender (E. Presley, V. Matson) | 8–?–56 | 10–20–56 | 1 |
| Love Me (J. Leiber, M. Stoller) | 9–1–56 | 11–17–56 | 2 |
| Too Much (L. Rosenberg, B. Weinman) | 9–2–56 | 1–26–57 | 1 |
| All Shook Up (O. Blackwell, E. Presley) | 1–12–57 | 4–6–57 | 1 |
| Teddy Bear (K. Mann, B. Lowe) | 1–24–57 | 6–24–57 | 1 |
| Jailhouse Rock (J. Leiber, M. Stoller) | 4–30–57 | 10–14–57 | 1 |
| Don't (J. Leiber, M. Stoller) | 9–6–57 | 1–27–58 | 1 |
| I Beg of You (R. McCoy, K. Owens) | 2–23–57 | 1–27–58 | 8 |
| Wear My Ring Around Your Neck (B. Carroll, R. Moody) | 2–1–58 | 4–21–58 | 2 |
| Hard Headed Woman (C. DeMetrius) | 1–15–58 | 6–30–58 | 1 |
| One Night (D. Bartholemew, P. King) | 2–23–57 | 11–3–58 | 4 |
| I Got Stung (A. Schroeder, D. Hill) | 6–11–58 | 11–3–58 | 8 |
| A Fool Such as I (B. Trader) | 6–10–58 | 3–23–59 | 2 |
| I Need Your Love Tonight (S. Wayne, B. Reichner) | 6–10–58 | 3–30–59 | 4 |

| | | | |
|---|---|---|---|
| A Big Hunk o' Love<br>(A. Schroeder, S. Wyche) | 6–10–58 | 7–6–59 | 1 |
| Stuck on You<br>(A. Schroeder, S. L. McFarland) | 3–21–60 | 4–4–60 | 1 |
| It's Now or Never<br>(A. Schroeder, W. Gold) | 4–3–60 | 7–18–60 | 1 |
| Are You Lonesome Tonight?<br>(R. Turk, L. Handman) | 4–4–60 | 11–14–60 | 1 |
| Surrender<br>(D. Pomus, M. Shuman) | 10–30–60 | 2–20–61 | 1 |
| I Feel So Bad<br>(C. Willis) | 3–12–61 | 5–15–61 | 5 |
| Little Sister<br>(D. Pomus, M. Shuman) | 6–26–61 | 8–21–61 | 5 |
| His Latest Flame<br>(D. Pomus, M. Shuman) | 6–26–61 | 8–28–61 | 4 |
| Can't Help Falling in Love<br>(H. Peretti, L. Creatore, C. Weiss) | 3–23–61 | 12–4–61 | 2 |
| Good Luck Charm<br>(A. Schroeder, W. Gold) | 10–15–61 | 3–17–62 | 1 |
| She's Not You<br>(D. Pomus, J. Leiber, M. Stoller) | 3–19–62 | 8–4–62 | 5 |
| Return to Sender<br>(O. Blackwell, W. Scott) | 3–?–62 | 10–20–62 | 2 |
| Devil in Disguise<br>(B. Giant, B. Baum, F. Kaye) | 5–26–63 | 6–29–63 | 3 |
| Bossa Nova Baby<br>(J. Leiber, M. Stoller) | 1–22–63 | 10–19–63 | 8 |
| Crying in the Chapel<br>(A. Glenn) | 10–31–60 | 4–24–65 | 3 |
| In the Ghetto<br>(S. Davis) | 1–21–69 | 5–3–69 | 3 |
| Suspicious Minds<br>(M. James) | 1–23–69 | 9–13–69 | 1 |
| Don't Cry Daddy<br>(S. Davis) | 1–15–69 | 11–29–69 | 6 |
| The Wonder of You<br>(T. B. Knight) | 2–19–70 | 5–16–70 | 9 |
| Burning Love<br>(D. Linde) | 3–28–72 | 8–19–72 | 2 |

## Films

| | | | |
|---|---|---|---|
| *Love Me Tender* | Twentieth Century-Fox | 1956 | 89 min.* |
| *Jailhouse Rock* | Metro-Goldwyn-Mayer | 1957 | 96 min. |
| *Loving You* | Paramount | 1957 | 101 min. |
| *King Creole* | Paramount | 1958 | 116 min. |
| *Flaming Star* | Twentieth Century-Fox | 1960 | 101 min. |
| *G.I. Blues* | Paramount | 1960 | 104 min. |
| *Blue Hawaii* | Paramount | 1961 | 101 min. |
| *Wild in the Country* | Twentieth Century-Fox | 1961 | 114 min. |
| *Follow That Dream* | United Artists | 1962 | 109 min. |
| *Kid Galahad* | United Artists | 1962 | 95 min. |
| *Girls! Girls! Girls!* | Paramount | 1962 | 106 min. |
| *It Happened at the World's Fair* | Metro-Goldwyn-Mayer | 1963 | 105 min. |
| *Fun in Acapulco* | Paramount | 1963 | 98 min. |
| *Kissin' Cousins* | Metro-Goldwyn-Mayer | 1964 | 96 min. |
| *Viva Las Vegas* | Metro-Goldwyn-Mayer | 1964 | 83 min. |
| *Roustabout* | Paramount | 1964 | 101 min. |
| *Girl Happy* | Metro-Goldwyn-Mayer | 1965 | 96 min. |
| *Tickle Me* | Allied Artists | 1965 | 90 min. |
| *Harum Scarum* | Metro-Goldwyn-Mayer | 1965 | 84 min. |
| *Frankie and Johnny* | United Artists | 1966 | 87 min. |
| *Paradise—Hawaiian Style* | Paramount | 1966 | 91 min. |
| *Spinout* | Metro-Goldwyn-Mayer | 1966 | 93 min. |
| *Double Trouble* | Metro-Goldwyn-Mayer | 1967 | 92 min. |
| *Easy Come, Easy Go* | Paramount | 1967 | 97 min. |
| *Clambake* | United Artists | 1967 | 98 min. |
| *Live a Little, Love a Little* | Metro-Goldwyn-Mayer | 1968 | 89 min. |
| *Speedway* | Metro-Goldwyn-Mayer | 1968 | 94 min. |
| *Stay Away, Joe* | Metro-Goldwyn-Mayer | 1968 | 101 min. |
| *Charro!* | National General Pictures | 1969 | 98 min. |
| *The Trouble with Girls* | Metro-Goldwyn-Mayer | 1969 | 104 min. |
| *Change of Habit* | Universal | 1969 | 93 min. |
| *Elvis . . . That's the Way It Is* | Metro-Goldwyn-Mayer | 1970 | 108 min. |
| *Elvis on Tour* | Metro-Goldwyn-Mayer | 1972 | 93 min. |

*The only film in which Elvis did not have top billing, and the only picture in which his character died

## Concert Tours

**1970**

| | |
|---|---|
| February 27–March 1 | Houston |
| September 9 | Phoenix |
| September 10 | St. Louis |
| September 11 | Detroit |
| September 12 | Miami |
| September 13 | Tampa |
| September 14 | Mobile |
| November 10 | Oakland |
| November 11 | Portland, Oreg. |
| November 12 | Seattle |
| November 13 | San Francisco |
| November 14 | Los Angeles |
| November 15 | San Diego |
| November 16 | Oklahoma City |
| November 17 | Denver |

**1971**

| | |
|---|---|
| November 5 | Minneapolis |
| November 6 | Cleveland |
| November 7 | Louisville |
| November 8 | Philadelphia |
| November 9 | Baltimore |
| November 10 | Boston |
| November 11 | Cincinnati |
| November 12 | Houston |
| November 13 | Dallas |
| November 14 | Tuscaloosa |
| November 15 | Kansas City |
| November 16 | Salt Lake City |

**1972**

| | |
|---|---|
| April 5 | Buffalo |
| April 6 | Detroit |
| April 7 | Dayton |
| April 8 | Knoxville |
| April 9 | Hampton Roads |
| April 10 | Richmond |
| April 11 | Roanoke |
| April 12 | Indianapolis |
| April 13 | Charlotte |

| | |
|---|---|
| April 14 | Greensboro |
| April 15 | Macon |
| April 16 | Jacksonville |
| April 17 | Little Rock |
| April 18 | San Antonio |
| April 19 | Albuquerque |
| June 9–11 | New York (Madison Square Garden) |
| June 12 | Fort Wayne |
| June 13 | Evansville |
| June 14–15 | Milwaukee |
| June 16–17 | Chicago |
| June 18 | Fort Worth |
| June 19 | Wichita |
| June 20 | Tulsa |
| November 8 | Lubbock |
| November 9 | Tucson |
| November 10 | El Paso |
| November 11 | Oakland |
| November 12–13 | San Bernardino |
| November 14–15 | Long Beach |
| November 17–18 | Honolulu |

**1973**

| | |
|---|---|
| January 14 | Honolulu* |
| June 20 | Mobile |
| June 21 | Atlanta |
| June 22–24 | Uniondale (Massau Memorial Coliseum) |
| June 25–26 | Pittsburgh |
| June 27 | Cincinnati |
| June 28 | St. Louis |
| June 29–30 | Atlanta |
| July 1 | Nashville |
| July 2 | Oklahoma City |

**1974**

| | |
|---|---|
| June 15–16 | Fort Worth |
| June 17–18 | Baton Rouge |
| June 19 | Amarillo |
| June 20 | Des Moines |
| June 21 | Cleveland |

* Worldwide Satellite Show, Honolulu International Center

| | |
|---|---|
| June 22 | Providence |
| June 23 | Philadelphia |
| June 24 | Niagara Falls |
| June 25 | Columbus |
| June 26 | Louisville |
| June 27 | Bloomington |
| June 28 | Milwaukee |
| June 29 | Kansas City |
| June 30–July 1 | Omaha |
| July 2 | Salt Lake City |

1975

| | |
|---|---|
| March 19 | Charlotte |
| March 20 | Johnson City |
| March 21 | Cincinnati |
| April 24 | Macon |
| April 25 | Jacksonville |
| April 26 | Tampa |
| April 27–28 | Lakeland |
| April 29 | Murfreesboro |
| April 30–May 2 | Atlanta |
| May 3 | Monroe |
| May 4 | Lake Charles |
| May 5 | Jackson |
| May 6–7 | Murfreesboro |
| May 30–June 1 | Huntsville |
| June 2 | Mobile |
| June 3 | Tuscaloosa |
| June 4–5 | Houston |
| June 6 | Dallas |
| June 7 | Shreveport |
| June 8–9 | Jackson |
| June 10 | Memphis |
| July 10 | Cleveland |
| July 11 | Charleston |
| July 12 | Niagara Falls |
| July 14–15 | Springfield |
| July 16 | New Haven |
| July 18 | Cleveland |
| July 18 | Uniondale |
| July 20 | Norfolk |
| July 22 | Asheville, N.C. |

| | |
|---|---|
| December 31 | Detroit[†] |

**1976**

| | |
|---|---|
| April 21 | Kansas City |
| April 22 | Omaha |
| April 23 | Denver |
| April 24 | San Diego |
| April 26 | Long Beach |
| April 28 | Seattle |
| April 29 | Spokane |
| June 24 | Syracuse |
| June 25 | Buffalo |
| June 26 | Rochester |
| June 27 | Syracuse |
| July 4 | Memphis |
| July 24 | Charleston |
| July 26 | Landover |
| July 27 | Providence |
| July 28 | Hartford |
| July 29 | Springfield |
| July 30 | New Haven |
| August 7–8 | Syracuse |
| August 31 | Macon |
| September 4 | Lakeland |
| October 14–15 | Chicago |
| October 16 | Duluth |
| October 17 | Minneapolis |
| October 18 | Sioux Falls |
| October 19 | Madison |
| October 20 | South Bend |
| October 21 | Kalamazoo |
| October 22 | Urbana, University of Illinois |
| October 23 | Cleveland |
| November 28 | Anaheim |
| November 29 | San Francisco |
| December 28 | Dallas |
| December 30 | Birmingham |

**1977**

| | |
|---|---|
| March 23 | Tempe, University of Arizona |

[†] Elvis earned $816,000 in one performance, believed to be the all-time record for a single performer anywhere

| | |
|---|---|
| March 24 | Amarillo |
| March 25–26 | Norman |
| April 20 | Columbia |
| April 21 | Greensboro |
| April 22 | Detroit |
| April 23 | Toledo |
| April 24 | Saginaw |
| April 27 | Milwaukee |
| April 30 | St. Paul |
| May 22 | Landover |
| May 23 | Providence |
| May 24 | Augusta |
| May 25 | Rochester |
| May 26–27 | Birmingham |
| May 28 | Philadelphia |
| May 29 | Baltimore[‡] |
| June 2 | Mobile |
| June 18 | Kansas City |
| June 25 | Cincinnati |

Tour canceled due to Elvis's death:

| | |
|---|---|
| August 17–18 | Portland, Maine |
| August 19 | Utica |
| August 20 | Syracuse |
| August 21 | Hartford |
| August 22 | Uniondale |
| August 23 | Lexington |
| August 24 | Roanoke |
| August 25 | Fayetteville |
| August 26 | Ashville, N.C. |
| August 27–28 | Memphis |

---

[‡]Elvis walked out on his audience for the first time in his career

## Television Appearances

Stage Show (with Tommy and Jimmy Dorsey) CBS
  January 28, 1956
  February 4, 1956
  February 11, 1956
  February 18, 1956
  March 17, 1956
  March 24, 1956

The Milton Berle Show (NBC)
  April 3, 1956
  June 5, 1956

The Steve Allen Show (NBC)
  July 1, 1956

Ed Sullivan's Toast of the Town (CBS)
  September 9, 1956
  October 28, 1956
  January 6, 1957

The Today Show (NBC)
  Excerpt from Elvis's press conference at Fort Dix, New Jersey, on completion of his U.S. Army tour of duty, March 4, 1960

The Frank Sinatra Timex Show (ABC)
  May 12, 1960

Singer Presents Elvis (NBC)
  December 3, 1968

Elvis: Aloha from Hawaii (NBC)
  April 4, 1973

## Club Appearances

Frontier Hotel, Las Vegas
  March 23–29, 1956

International Hotel, Las Vegas
  July 31–August 28, 1969
  January 26–February 23, 1970
  August 30–September 7, 1970
  January 26–February 23, 1971
  August 9–September 6, 1971
  January 26–February 23, 1972
  August 4–September 4, 1972

Sahara Tahoe, Lake Tahoe
  July 20–August 2, 1971
  May 4–20, 1973
  May 16–26, 1974
  October 11–14, 1974
  April 30–May 9, 1976

Las Vegas Hilton, Las Vegas
  January 26–February 23, 1973
  August 6–September 3, 1973
  January 26–February 9, 1974
  August 20–September 2, 1974
  March 18–31, 1975
  August 18–September 2, 1975
  December 2–15, 1975
  August 20–September 1, 1976*
  December 1–12, 1976

* canceled after three nights due to illness